*Befriending the Mind*

also by Doug Kraft

Centering Home

Buddha's Map

Beginning the Journey

Kindness and Wisdom Practice

Meditator's Field Guide

# Befriending the Mind:

## Easing into the
## Heart of Awakening

# Doug Kraft

Easing Awake Books

ISBN 13: 978-0-9986936-8-2 paperback
ISBN 13: 978-0-9986936-9-9 e-book

Cover photo by Spencer Pugh
Hammock image on p. 4 by Austin Schmid.
Both photos through https://www.unsplash.com.

Unless noted otherwise, sutta translations are from Bhikkhu
Bodhi through Wisdom Publications (199 Elm Street,
Sommerville, MA 02144).

Printed in the United States
5 4 3 2 1

# Contents

## *Inner Landscape*

# Introduction:

# Don't Stand in a Hammock

I've seen meditators put too much of the wrong kind of effort into their practice. They think the mind needs to be controlled, disciplined, shaped, or trained. This is like trying to stand up in a hammock: it's tiring, destabilizing, difficult to do, and completely unnecessary.

There is a natural kindness and intelligence in the mind-heart that can easily be obscured. As meditators, our job is not to get a grip on the mind but to discover the clarity and wisdom that is inherent in it. This may take effort and discipline, but wise effort seeks not to control, it seeks to reveal.

To be sure, the mind can go out of control in many ways. Sometimes the mind is like a drunken coyote howling at the moon with more enthusiasm than it knows what to do with. Sometimes it's like a snail sliding across a large gymnasium in the dead of night not knowing where it is, where it's going, or where to find the energy to keep moving through the gloom.

During these times we naturally yearn for a little stability, peace, vitality, clarity, or uplift. To get these, we may be tempted to take charge and will them onto the mind. However, as everyone who has broken a New Year's resolution knows, habit is stronger than will. Willpower may work for a few hours or a few days — but in the long run, it's hard to sustain. And as the spiritual teacher Adyashanti puts it: "If we oppose the mind, we will be at war forever."

Rather than trying to rule over the mind-heart, we can befriend it — open up to it with kindness, get to know it better, see how it operates.

As we befriend the mind-heart, we see that a restless mind has too much energy. It tries to burn off excess vim by howling, chattering, or running around. It wants what we want. Its heart is in the right place, but its strategy is unwise. Forcing quiet onto an over-energized mind is like yelling at a rambunctious child to sit down and shut up: the scolding agitates it even more.

On the other hand, the sluggish mind has the opposite problem: not enough energy. It has a different kind of tension that feels thick, like cold molasses. It tries to rejuvenate by slowing down and conserving energy. It wants vitality but doesn't know where to find it. Telling it to perk up and do what needs to be done can make the situation worse by demanding more energy. Like standing in a hammock, it is tiring.

To befriend the mind-heart, we look past its stories and justifications to attend to the underlying feeling tones and textures. We can take them to heart, relate to them wisely, listen to them compassionately. We can soothe, ground, inspire, and relax. This is like settling into a hammock. The tension eases, the gloom dissipates, peace and clarity emerge.

A traditional Buddhist metaphor for this process is the parting of storm clouds — the sun shines through and we notice the openness of the sky itself. The sun is always shining. The sky is always spacious. Clouds can obscure the luminous expansiveness, but these qualities are always present. We don't create them. If we had to create peace, vitality, or wisdom, they would not last. Instead, we discover what was previously hidden.

This is the wisdom of the uncontrolled mind.

# Uncontrolled Middle Way

Uncontrolled does not mean that the mind has gone nuts. The out-of-control mind is scattered by unconscious forces, reactivity, and bad habits. On the other hand, the controlled mind is limited by our current understandings. The uncontrolled mind is neither scattered nor limited. It's a middle way. Like the sky on a clear day, it's calm and has limitless possibilities.

The thesis of this book is that what we truly seek is already here, though it may be obscured. Discovering our natural peace and vitality is a middle way that is neither domineering nor out of control. This path exposes a natural mind-heart that is peaceful, luminous, patient, intelligent, kind, wise, gentle, agendaless, and so quiet it does nothing to draw attention. Attuning to it could be called "easing awake."

I have been exploring, teaching, and writing about easing awake for years. The first time I was invited to lead a nine-day retreat, I made a list of dhamma talk topics and arranged them in the order in which they were most likely to arise in a yogi's experience. The sequence was:

- How to meditate: the mechanics of the practice
- How to engage so-called "hindrances" as tools for insight and wisdom
- How this practice resonates with the larger Buddha dhamma
- Using dependent origination (aka dependent co-arising) as a practical tool
- How stages of meditation (jhānas) unfold naturally
- Understanding selflessness and nondual awareness
- Integrating meditation into daily life

In subsequent years, I wrote new talks on the same themes, using different illustrations, approaches, subtopics, and lengths of time on any given topic.

The format for these talks was lecture followed by questions and answers. This was how much of the dhamma had been transmitted to me. But I began to suspect this was not the most dynamic and effective learning style. People absorb more when they engage material deeply, actively, and experientially rather than when they just listen passively.

So I shifted from delivering monologues to presenting exercises, guided experiences, and engaged discussions. I still wanted to make the old-style lecture material available in written form because that format is helpful for some topics and for some people. Yogis who found the old style helpful could have my best thoughts in hand before, during, and after the retreat. This collection would be a kind of retreat companion.

I looked through the talks I had given over the years and chose the ones I thought were the best on each topic. As I edited them, I realized that the collection might be useful in other settings too. So I gathered them into the book you are holding. The order of chapters roughly follows my original sequence, with a few extras here and there. I split the chapters up into three sections:

- Befriending the mind-heart, with all its hindrances and quirks
- The inner landscape of our own experience, along with what the Buddha and modern science have to say about that experience
- Luminous nondual awareness

A small percentage of the material in the following pages first appeared in previous books of mine and is repeated in this book for the sake of continuity and clarity.

I hope you find these writings helpful in befriending what is inherent in all of us: the luminous, spacious wisdom of the uncontrolled mind.

# Befriending

If the mind-heart is so wise and wonderful, how come we are so vulnerable to confusion, delusion, and neurosis? To answer this, we must look closely at the nature of the mind itself and the confusion that distracts, misguides, and hinders us. And before we look at hindrances, it would be valuable to see the positive role of vulnerability in meditation and in life. These are the topics of this section.

# 1

# Vulnerability

Has life ever taken you to the edge of what you can manage, and then kept right on going without slowing down?

*In mid-October of 1982, my wife, Erika, almost died. She was almost nine months into our second pregnancy. We were monitoring possible Rh blood incompatibility between her and the fetus. Otherwise things were healthy.*

*At a routine pre-natal exam, our family doctor said he wanted her to see an ob-gyn physician immediately. It turned out she had a more serious condition called preeclampsia. Eclampsia is the Greek word for lightning. That is how it comes on: fast with potentially devastating effects. There aren't many treatment options. The only possible cure was to deliver the baby.*

*Fortunately, our doctors recognized what was going on. And fortunately, we were almost full-term, so the risk of delivering the baby was minimal. They sent us straight to the hospital delivery room. "No," our doctor said. "Don't go home to get clothes first. I'll meet you at the hospital."*

*As Erika was being prepped, lightning struck. Her blood pressure shot up to 280 over something. Organ systems began to shut down. "She's about to have a seizure," the doctor said.*

*They were able to stabilize her. It was a struggle. But in the wee hours of the morning, they were ready for an emergency cesarean section. The nurses tried to get me out of the operating room. The doctor looked at me for a moment, then turned to the nurses. "He's okay," the doctor said. "He's been calm through this. He can stay."*

*I was so grateful.*

*A short while later they took a dark mass from Erika's body that didn't look like anything I had ever imagined. But I knew it was our child. He took a breath and turned from grey to pink for a moment.*

*The operating room began to turn like a slow-motion carousel on the side of a hill. I was determined not to faint and draw attention away from Erika and the baby. I sat on a stool as they brought the baby over to a scale next to me. One of the doctors examined him. "He's fine. Apgar score of nine." (The Apgar is a ten-point scale used to rapidly assess the vitality of a newborn.)*

*The nurse wrapped him up and sent him off to the nursery so the medical team could focus on putting Erika back together.*

*Ten minutes later they wheeled her out of the room. The doctor looked back at me, "She's going to be okay. She'll be out for a while and will probably feel pretty awful when she wakes up. But she's out of the woods. She'll be fine."*

*Somehow I found my way to the nursery. The nurses set me up in a big rocking chair. Then they brought over a swaddled baby who fit in the palms of my two hands. I was so grateful to feel his tiny body.*

*When our first son, Nathan, was born five years earlier, he had trouble breathing and was quickly sent off to a hospital an hour and a half away that had a neonatal intensive care unit. When I got there the next morning, he was like a hedgehog bristling with tubes, wires, and medical equipment. It was hard to snuggle with him.*

*So with our second son, I was so grateful to be handed a little body wrapped in nothing but a blanket.*

*Erika and I both liked the name Damon, but we wanted to meet him before we settled on a name.*

*His eyes were wide open looking up at me. I looked down at him. "You're Damon," I said. It felt right.*

*Then we were just there. Looking at each other.*

*After a few minutes — or maybe a few hours, I couldn't tell — I noticed that the sky outside the window was turning pink. Dawn.*

Nathan and my mother-in-law were probably waking up and wondering what was going on. I decided to go home and fill them in.

When I pulled into the driveway, Nathan came running out of the house carrying a doll by the foot. Erika and I had gotten it for him as a present. We had wrapped it up and left it with my mother-in-law to give to him when his brother came out.

I filled him in on the essentials — he had a new baby brother, it had been a rough delivery, but everyone was okay now. And we were going to the Pancake House to celebrate.

Back home an hour later I decided to take a nap before going back to the hospital. I'd been up for 30 hours. I sat down on the bed and pulled out my journal. I closed my eyes and put myself back into that nursery when Damon and I had first gazed into each other's eyes. I recalled as clearly as I could the actual words that had gone through my mind, and jotted them down so I could tell him years later. This is what I wrote:

"Welcome, little friend, little being entrusted to our care. I just keep thinking, 'Welcome little friend.'

"Where did you come from, you with the stars in your hair and the ocean depths in your brown eyes? Such tiny fingers. Such a large soul.

"Wherever you came from, you are here now. This is the earth, and I'll be your daddy this time. In the years ahead, we will laugh and cry and no doubt quarrel together. We will watch our lives unfold.

"But somehow, at this moment, when your body is so soft and new to the world, we seem closer to who we truly are together. And the love in it nearly overwhelms me.

"Do you understand this? Do you know what I'm thinking? Have we met before? This feels more like a reunion than a meeting of strangers.

"How can such a little being affect me so, unless the essence is not what the doctors and nurses weigh and measure.

"There is mystery here — something much bigger than I can capture. And I'm truly grateful for that.

"Welcome, little friend."

## Loving Our Vulnerability

The events of mid-October 1982 touched and moved me because I was so vulnerable. I wasn't frightened. Fear requires anticipating negative consequences and choosing to fight against them. But there was no time to anticipate, and life had overwhelmed my defenses. I couldn't have resisted if I'd tried.

I was just present, dealing only with the moment. That's all I could manage. That's why the doctor saw me as calm. I was incredibly vulnerable yet had no fear. Fear came later when I had time to think about all the things that might have happened.

Usually we have time to anticipate and choose how to relate to our experience. We can open a little more or shy away. But on that day, life took over and ripped me open. Thankfully.

Vulnerability has negative connotations because it can leave us feeling weak and more susceptible to hurt, grief, disappointment, depression, loneliness, failure, and more. But vulnerability also makes us more susceptible to tenderness, gratitude, love, surprise, growth, and change.

When we sit down to meditate, go off on retreat, or just contemplate life in the wee hours of the morning, what are we looking for? Perhaps a little love, kindness, peace, contentment, serenity, wisdom, insight, equanimity, joy, or awakening? None of these are possible without vulnerability.

We'd like to open up without risk, break through without breakage, awaken without being disturbed. But it's a package deal. We can't have one without the other because they all require vulnerability.

A yogi sent me a link to a TED talk by Brené Brown on vulnerability.[1] She describes herself as a social scientist–researcher–storyteller. In pouring through hundreds of stories people had sent her about difficult situations in their lives, she found that those who

---

[1] https://www.ted.com/talks/brene_brown_on_vulnerability

did well with their vulnerability had heartfully embraced it. Those who didn't do well had collapsed into guilt and shame.

As she dug more deeply, she saw that those who embraced their vulnerability felt worthy of love. Those who contracted into shame felt unworthy.

How about you? Do you feel worthy?...

Come on. We are all worthy of love. How could it be otherwise? We are worthy not because of *who* we are. We are worthy not because of *what* we do. We are worthy simply *because we are*. We have arisen out of this intricate weaving of matter, energy, and spirit that is the web of life itself. We are part of it all. We belong here. This is our home. We are all worthy of love because we are all a part of everything.

But the people and events in our lives may have taught us otherwise. Particularly in the West where achievement-oriented styles of childrearing too often foster self-hatred, many of us have learned otherwise. All of us probably have some unworthiness to unlearn.

It's valuable to set aside time for this unlearning; time for rediscovering our natural, humble worthiness; time for deepening our capacities for embracing vulnerability and for opening to the grace and wisdom that come with these qualities. Such time might include quiet conversation with a friend, mentor, counselor, or trusted guide. It might include solitary walks in nature. It might include daily meditation. I have found extended meditation retreats particularly helpful because they combine all these elements.

When I go on retreat, I'm looking for a place that stirs my natural vulnerability to awakening. When I'm leading a retreat, I try to provide this for others.

Don't get me wrong. I don't try to beat hearts open like all those encounter groups I joined years ago. I don't schedule near-death experiences or observations of loved ones in surgery. I don't even bring in babies to snuggle.

My retreat strategy is gentle. It begins with a quiet facility, hopefully with access to nature. It provides good food, comfortable rooms, and a gentle setting that is disarming. Rather than confront our defenses, this strategy removes distractions. It replaces idle conversation with silence. It replaces cell phones, computers, books, and entertainment with quiet.

In this setting we're invited to confront ourselves. Over and over we're encouraged to sit down on a cushion or comfortable chair and close our eyes. Then we're left alone and unchaperoned with our mind.

Sometimes the mind is lovely, expansive, and sweet. Sometimes it's crazy. Sometimes it's blah. The hard-earned wisdom I've learned about deepening our connection with life is to embrace our tenderness — practice loving our vulnerability.

This may mean different things at different times. When we feel bummed, loving our vulnerability means having compassion and kindness for those tender spots. When we feel expansive or joyful, loving our vulnerability means savoring these wholesome qualities and letting them soften us. When we feel humdrum, loving our vulnerability means loving the common, ordinary, earthiness of our lives.

The Buddha hints at these qualities throughout the *Sutta Nipata* by saying, "You are not better than anyone else. You are not worse than anyone else. And you are not the same as anyone else."[2]

Your sensitivity is expressed in unique ways. Love this vulnerability.

## Practice

I have found two interacting practices particularly helpful. They are a bedrock that supports the entire path. As they deepen, they

---

[2] "One should not take oneself as 'equal' or think of oneself as 'inferior' or 'superior.'" *Sutta Nipāta* 4.5 (PTS Sn 799), trans. Bhikkhu Bodhi, *Suttanipāta.* (Somerville MA, Wisdom Publication, 2017), p. 296.

unfold and shift to take advantage of what we've learned. I have written about these extensively in *Buddha's Map*[3] and *Meditator's Field Guide,* so I'll just offer a quick review here. [4]

## Preparation

Before meditating, it is helpful to find a relatively quiet place to sit comfortably. Sit upright if possible — lounging invites the body and mind to go to sleep rather than wake up. But the posture should be comfortable. Cushions or chairs are both fine. Sitting cross-legged isn't required. A posture that is familiar to your body will be less distracting and more helpful than one that is uncomfortable.

## Mettā

To start the actual meditation, remember what happiness feels like. Perhaps you recently accomplished something that left you feeling great. Perhaps it was the soft happiness of holding a small animal that cuddled into you. Perhaps it was the selfless joy of watching a child play. Perhaps it was the serenity of watching a sunset by the ocean.

All of us have felt happy at times — many times — in our lives. The feeling may vary depending on our temperament, history, conditioning, and circumstance. The flavor of happiness is not important: kindness, joy, compassion, equanimity, gratitude – any uplifted quality that has little tension in it or that naturally reduces tension.

This is where this meditation practice begins — not so much with the memory of the situation but with the feeling itself. It's like a glowing in the center of your chest.

To begin, put an image of yourself in your heart. Some people visualize easily; others don't. It's not important that you clearly visualize. Just imagine holding yourself gently in the center of your chest.

---

[3] Doug Kraft, *Buddha's Map,* (Carmichael, CA: Easing Awake Books, 2017).
[4] Doug Kraft, *Meditator's Field Guide* (Carmichael, CA: Easing Awake Books, 2017).

Then send yourself a wish for happiness or well-being. "May I be happy." "May I be peaceful." "May I feel safe and secure." "May I feel ease throughout my day." Any uplifted state is fine.

The phrases are a way of priming the pump — they evoke the feeling. As it arises, shift your attention to the feeling itself.

Sooner or later the feeling will fade. When it does, repeat a phrase. It's not helpful to repeat it rapidly — this makes the phrase feel mechanical. Rather, say the phrase sincerely, and rest for a few moments with the feeling it evokes. Then repeat it again.

As you do this, three things arise in the mind-heart: the person to whom you are wishing happiness (yourself), the mental phrase, and the feeling. About 70 percent of your attention should be on the feeling, 20 to 25 percent on the person (yourself), and just a little on the phrase used to evoke the feeling.

It is difficult to force a feeling to arise — and unwise to even try. So if the feeling is not present, let 70 percent of your attention rest on your intention to send uplifted qualities to yourself. The sincerity of your intention creates the environment in which the feeling itself can arise. Sometimes this takes patience.

After about ten minutes, switch the person to whom you are sending kind wishes. Rather than sending kindness to yourself, send it to a "spiritual friend."

## Spiritual Friend

A spiritual friend is a living person to whom you find it very easy to wish the best. It might be a favorite teacher who always has your highest interests at heart. It might be an aunt or uncle who always looks out for you. It might be a small child who opens your heart.

A partner is not a good choice for a spiritual friend. You may have a lot of love for him or her, but primary relationships are usually complex. For the purpose of meditation training, simple is better. For the same reason, a teenage son or daughter is probably not a good choice — those relationships have too many textures. A person you find physically attractive is not a good choice either.

Physical attraction can become thick, complicated, and distracting. You want the meditation to be light, easy, and uncomplicated.

Once you have settled on a good spiritual friend, stick with that person. If you switch from one person to another, the practice won't be able to ripen or deepen. And if you stay with one person in your meditation, the other people in your life will benefit even without being the explicit focus of your sitting practice.

So each time you sit down to practice, send well wishes to yourself for 10 minutes. Then switch to your same chosen spiritual friend.

### The Six Rs

Metta — the practice of sending kindness, well-being, or other uplifted intentions — is the storefront. It is something wholesome to occupy the mind-heart. A second practice in the backroom is just as important — if not more important. It's called the Six Rs. It is a paint-by-the-number implementation of what the Buddha meant by right effort. These two practices work intimately together as one.

As you send well-wishing to yourself or your spiritual friend, other things will occur uninvited. Thoughts, images, sensations, and emotions waltz in. This is not your intention, but the mind has a mind of its own.

As long as you're still with the feeling of well-wishing, kindness, or peace, don't be concerned about these intrusions. Let them float in the background, as it were, without doing anything about them.

But sooner or later, a distraction will hijack your attention completely. You won't see this coming. One moment you'll be sending kindness. The next thing you know, you're rehearsing a conversation, planning your day, reminiscing about yesterday, or otherwise attending to something other than the object of your meditation.

This is great news! Now you get to use the second meditation practice. This is a powerful practice that can only be used when the mind wanders. Now's your chance!

The drifting mind is a symptom of tension disturbing your underlying peace. This side of enlightenment, we all have many tensions. The distraction points one out — it shows exactly where it is so that you can release it skillfully. This is so helpful.

The only trick is to release the tension wisely. An unwise way is to condemn yourself, "Oh, I can't do this!" That criticism creates more tension and destabilizes the mind further. It's a form of aversion. Another unwise strategy is to buckle down and try harder to control the mind. This too creates more tension and restlessness. It's a form of greed.

A better approach is employing a technique known as the Six Rs. These are as follows:

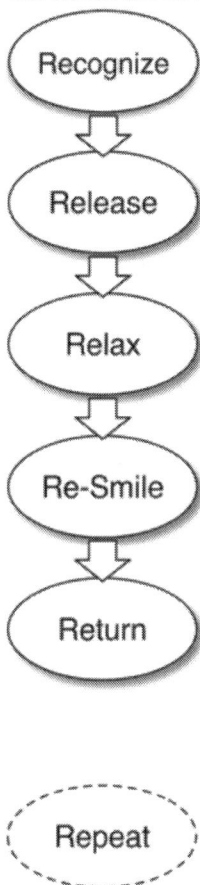

**1. Recognize** where your attention has gone. In time it will be clear that wisdom moved your attention to that particular place. What that wisdom is may not be clear right now. That's fine. All you need to do is recognize where your attention went.

**2. Release** your grip on the distraction. Let it be. Don't push it away or hold onto it. Release the hold it has on your attention or that your attention has on it.

**3. Relax**. Let go of any tension in your mind or body. You don't have to search for tension like an enthusiastic detective. Just relax. That's enough.

**4. Re-Smile**, or smile again. Allow a higher state — any uplifted state — to come into the mind-heart. Having a good sense of humor about how the mind drifts is helpful. So, smile.

**5. Return**. Now take the relaxed mind-heart and this brighter, lighter state back to your object of meditation.

Recognize

Release

Relax

Re-Smile

Return

Repeat

**6. Repeat**. The repetition will happen automatically if you continue meditating — that is to say, the mind will wander again and again. If you haven't released all the tension from a particular distraction, that's fine. It will simply come up again until you have. You can relax in confidence that the mind-heart will let you know if there's more to relax.

This Six-R process contains the practical essence of the Buddha's Four Noble Truths and Eightfold Path. It is also what he meant by wise effort or effort without strain or tension. Using the Six Rs puts us squarely on the path he described.

## Time

To start, 30 minutes per sitting is adequate, though 45 minutes or more will serve you better. It takes a little time to settle into the practice. If you meditate a little longer, the practice may go deeper more quickly.

## Sitting Still

Once you get comfortable, try not to move throughout this period of time. If the mind insists on moving, Six-R the tension in the insistence. The Six Rs are very helpful in letting the mind release tension and find deeper ease.

Of course, if pain arises from genuine physical harm, you will want to adjust your posture. The way to tell if you should adjust is to notice what happens when you get up from sitting. If the pain goes away very quickly, it was probably not caused by anything harmful. If the painful feeling returns when you sit next, try to remain still and Six-R the tightness that arises around the pain. If, on the other hand, when you get up the pain lingers, it is best not to sit in that posture in the future.

The Buddha saw that craving or tightness is the root of all suffering. It also gives rise to distractions. So softening the tightness goes to the core of his teaching and practice.

# Hindrances

When we sit down and close our eyes, it's hard to know what will show up in the mind-heart field. Unwelcome phenomena are traditionally called "hindrances." The Six Rs are a wise response to them. However, whether we've been meditating for five minutes or 50 years, hindrances are likely to continue to arise. How we relate to them often shapes our entire meditation practice. So in the next few chapters, we'll have a look at ways to befriend these intrusions.

# 2

# The Demon's Blessing

*Jacob was jealous of his big brother, Esau. Esau always got better stuff. In fact, Esau was going to get the entire family inheritance: sheep, goats, tents… everything. In ancient times, that was the rule: the oldest gets it all.*

*Their father, Isaac, was 180 years old, according to legends: old, blind, and maybe a little feeble. So Jacob was able to trick his father into giving him the inheritance.*

*To get his birthright, Esau would have to kill Jacob. And he was enraged enough to do just that. So Jacob ran for his life. He found safe haven in a neighboring country. He took up shepherding, got married, and began to raise a family: he prospered.*

*He was tempted to forget about Esau and his past. But his heart nudged him to face his trickery and reconcile with his brother. So he packed his tents; gathered his family, servants, and flocks; and began the journey back to the homeland. It took weeks.*

*Late one afternoon they came to the Jabbok River – less than a day's walk from the old homestead. He set up camp for the night beside the river.*

*Then, in the dead of the night, Jacob awoke. The hair on the back of his neck was standing on end. There was something in the camp. Was it Esau come to kill him? Was it a wild beast? Was it a demon? Jacob couldn't tell.*

What would you have done?

*Jacob roused his household and sent them across the ford of the Jabbok toward the homestead. Then, alone, unarmed, in the black of night, and with no possibility of help, he went back into his abandoned camp.*

*Something grabbed him and threw him to the ground. Jacob grabbed its leg. Together they grappled in the dark. Jacob didn't prevail — but it didn't beat him either. Their struggle continued.*

*When the eastern sky turned grey with a hint of dawn it spoke, "Release me, for I must go."*

*Jacob said, "No."*

*The entity leaned over and with one finger dislocated Jacob's hip. Wow! Jacob realized this being was more powerful than it had let on! With one finger it had popped his leg out of its socket. It hurt!*

*It said, "Release me, for I must go."*

What would you have done?

*Jacob said, "No."*

*"What must I do to get you to release me?"*

*Jacob answered, "You must give me your blessing."*

*The demon turned out to be an angel. It said, "Your name shall no longer be 'Jacob.' You shall be known as 'Israel,' and from you shall descend an entire nation."*

*At that time and in that culture, that was the highest blessing one could receive.*

*So Jacob released the angel. It left. And Jacob limped into the sunrise.*

— Genesis 32:24–32

# Hindrances

On retreat I often spend the first day wrestling with demons. When I'm practicing at home, they like to visit me regularly. They may not be powerful enough to dislocate my hip, but they are good at dislocating my equanimity. And they are bold enough to come out in the broad daylight rather than wait for the dead of night. Their techniques may not be headlocks and half-nelsons, but they don't mind perturbing me with doubts, poking me with restlessness, dulling me with lullabies, and disrupting me with endless patter.

While Tibetan Buddhism often calls these disruptions "demons," Theravada Buddhism uses a more genteel term, *nīvaraṇa,* which means "hindrances." *Nīvaraṇa* are things that hinder our meditative progress.

As we meditate, we become familiar with a wide variety of hindrances. They are the energies that rise out of our depths — often the unseen aspects of our being. Like angels, they are messengers from beyond our normal awareness. Like oracles, their messages can be wise but cryptic and not easy to decipher. If the messages don't fit our fancy, do we kill the messenger? Do we scold it and say, "If you can't say something nice, don't say anything at all"? Do we blindly give in to a surface understanding and say, "Yeah. I knew I was a bad meditator"? Or do we listen with open minds and hearts and learn?

How we engage hindrances is the most important aspect of meditation training.

If we treat hindrances as demons to be conquered or corralled, we'll be locked in an endless struggle. But if we treat them as angels with wisdom to bestow, they can be a blessing.

To understand the gifts they offer, let's first look how hindrances can be a problem. Then we'll look broadly at them from three perspectives: (1) as crossed intentions, (2) as angels with Asperger's, and (3) as a split between self and other. Finally, in the next chapter, we'll look at specific hindrances and how to relate to each skillfully. Wisely engaging hindrances brings forth the gifts they can bestow.

## What's the Problem?

Before we get to specific hindrances, let's start with the question, "What's the problem with hindrances?"

The problem is distortion. At the core of every hindrance is tension: we want something, we don't want something, or we're confused about something — liking, aversion, or confusion. That tension distorts thinking, perception, and decision-making. That is why hindrances have been called "demons," "defilements," "taints," "cankers," "effluences," and the like: they muddy the mind and heart.

But the distortion itself is just an innocent biological reaction. Rather than give it a moralistic name, I prefer a functional label: "distortion."

A hindrance shows us where the mind-heart is distorted. The *Pāli* term *nīvaraṇa* literally means "covering" or "veil." A hindrance covers an underlying truth about what's happening. That is the bad news. The good news is a hindrance shows us exactly where the truth can be found: beneath that covering or veil. The angelic messenger is pointing it out.

It's up to us to lift that cover and see what's there. We Recognize the hindrance and the tightness in it. It's best not to get involved in the storyline — that's a dead end. Instead we just notice the tension in it. Release it. Relax. Smile (or Re-Smile). Return to radiating uplifted states And Repeat as often as our attention gets hijacked. (See pp. "The Six Rs," 17-19).

That is how to lift the cover. It works very well… most of the time. However, sometimes we Six-R over and over, and the same hindrance keeps returning — sometimes with vigor. Then we may need to lightly investigate and see if we're missing something. Without going into the story, we can spend more time with the Recognize step. We may notice the distraction more fully and the quality of the awareness that is noticing — is it open, tight, rushed, sluggish, or something else?

# Crossed Intentions

Sometimes we miss a crossed intention that invited the hindrance.

At first a hindrance may seem like a nuisance disrupting a pleasant afternoon, a demon sneaking in under the cover of night, or an unshaven guest who arriving at the dinner table unannounced. We think, "I didn't invite them."

But we did. *Nothing pops into our minds without an invitation.* During quiet moments of meditation or peaceful walks through the fields, these distractions come at our beckoning. A summons was issued from the psychophysical energy system in which we live. Hindrances show up because some part of us invited them.

If we don't remember enticing these creatures, then their appearance is an opportunity to explore parts of our system we've lost touch with. It's a chance to peer into dusty corners of our psyche.

For example, imagine Jacob's internal conflicts: homesickness, fear of Esau's anger, guilt for ripping him off, anger at his father for favoring Esau, resentment at a culture that gave all the goodies to the oldest, contriteness for breaking the laws, pride in his success, worry about what his family thought, trepidation about the kind of welcome he might receive... He had ample material for nightmares filled with demons. In fact, a modern retelling of the story might set this wrestling match in a bad dream.

We rarely have only one single intention. Usually we have many operating at once. Some we recognize, some we try to ignore. Many conflict with one another. They populate our dreams and our quiet waking moments.

In meditation we may go over and over a verbal wrestling match with our boss. "Go away," we say to those thoughts. "I'm tired of fighting these thoughts." But it may also be true that we'd like to win the fight and want some well-honed zingers rehearsed and ready to fire. We have crossed intentions.

Once I spent three days on a retreat designing a desk lamp. I kept telling myself I'd rather be meditating now, but part of me wanted the satisfaction of creating a lovely design. And part of me wanted a distraction from hours of futile attempts to focus my mind.

One of the reasons we have hindrances is mixed intentions. The hindrances will keep coming back until we see each intention clearly and Six-R them all. Hindrances show us distortions in our system that need wise attention.

So if you feel dogged by a recurrent hindrance, ask gently if you have crossed intentions. As you notice one, gently Recognize, Release, Relax, Re-smile, Return to sending out mettā, and Repeat as often as needed.

On the other hand, there are some hindrances we just don't like: we have no mixed intentions. We want them gone, period. That disliking is also an unwitting invitation: a cause or condition that draws them forth.

The rule is we get what we put our energy into.[5] If we invest in liking, that draws a hindrance. If we invest in disliking, that also invites a hindrance. If we invest in ignoring, that invites a hindrance.

# Angels with Asperger's

Another way to look at hindrances is as teachers. We can see them as guides from beyond who knows us well and can point out clandestine tension. Rather than view hindrances as troublemakers or crossed intentions, we can view them as wise teachers.

*I started lessons with my first piano teacher when I was in second grade and continued with her through Junior High. By then it was clear to my mother that I was deeply motivated. So she found a better teacher for me at a local conservatory. His name was Walter Giannini.*

*For the first nine months with Mr. Giannini I did nothing but exercises to build up my hands and coordination. We started with the Hannon School of Velocity and worked through Czerny, Scarlatti, and other classical training methods without looking at one actual piece of music.*

*But within a year and a half he had me playing Debussy and Gershwin preludes that previously I hadn't dreamed I could master.*

*Part of his talent was recognizing my motivations, weaknesses, and strengths. He was able to push me to the edge of what I could do without pushing me over that edge. It was a delicate balance. But he was sensitive and masterful.*

---

[5] The Buddha said it this way: "Whatever a monk frequently thinks and ponders upon, that will become the inclination of the mind." *Majjhima Nikāya* 19.6.

*Nevertheless, I had to do the work. He could only show me what to work on and offer tips, but I had to practice.*

The difference between Walter Giannini as a piano teacher and hindrances as spiritual teachers is that Mr. Giannini had a great personal sensitivity and social intelligence. Hindrances, by contrast, are angels with Asperger's syndrome: they don't understand social cues. They're not sensitive to our likes and dislikes, personality and mood, preferences and peeves. They just point out where we're out of balance. If we're tired or frustrated or don't feel like looking at those difficulties, it seems like they are rubbing our noses in the dirt.

However, if we are truly ready to move along quickly, they are wonderful guides, trainers, and even friends.

For me, a friend is someone who is able to call me on my games. A friend is someone who has the clarity, kindness, and willingness to say, "Doug, you're deluded on this one." If they can say that honestly and wisely, then I know I can trust them.

Hindrances have no problem showing us we're deluded — they're just clueless about social niceties.

Would you rather have someone politely say you're brilliant when you're confused, or have them show you that you're deluded when you think you're brilliant?

# Split Between Self and Other

We've looked at hindrances as crossed intentions and as guides, trainers, and friends. We can also view hindrances as a split between self and other. To see them as a split, let's look at their family tree: how they relate to one another and where they got started.

### Tanhā

In the beginning was the great-grandparent of all hindrances, the primal source of our unhappiness, the goddess of our discontent. Its name is…?

In *Pāli*, its name sounds like a flourish of trumpets: *Taṇhā*! The term literally means "thirst." It is most often translated as "craving."

*Taṇhā* can be as brash as a brass band. Or it can be as subtle as a disturbance in the Force — a quiet fluctuation in our equanimity. It runs the spectrum from a raving demon to a subtle thickening of mood.

*Taṇhā* is a preverbal, preconceptual, reflexive tightening. It's the gripping of our hands on the steering wheel when a driver cuts us off, the sudden focus on someone attractive, the quiet pining for a little more free time, the frustrations at the jingle in our mind.

### Self and Other

If we relax taṇhā, it dissipates. If we don't, it begets two children: Self and Other. They dearly love one another. Without Other there is no Self and without Self there is no Other.

The sense of self and other, of "me" perceiving something "out there," is so familiar that we may think it's basic to life. But it's not. In our deepest, purest experience there is just the flow of phenomena: experiences arise and pass.

But when taṇhā gets strong, it divides experience into categories: "This is me. This is not me." "This is mine. This is not mine." "This is myself. This is not myself."

The Buddha offered a very simple meditative tool to use when we get stuck in a hindrance. Ask, "Is this me? Is this mine? Is this myself?" The question is not one to figure out. It directs our awareness to take a closer look and see directly.

Here's a simple exercise:

Notice your sense of self. Where does it reside in the body? For most people, our feet are "down there" — our self looks down at our feet. Likewise our knees and our belly seem to be "down" below the center of the self.

The top of the head seems to be "up there."

The self that looks down at the knees and up at the crown, feels to be somewhere in between.

So close your eyes and see if you can locate the center of the self.

For most people, it is in the middle of the head perhaps about the level of the eyes or a little lower. From here we look out into the world or listen out for the sounds of the world.

This location of self is somewhat arbitrary and can be different for different people. For some it's more in the chest.

What's important is not to think where it should be, but to feel where it seems to be.

Once you have found it, bring your attention to it. Let the awareness seep into the center of the self. You'll probably notice some tension there.

Now allow that tension to soften. See what happens as it relaxes.

Some people may begin to feel a little spacious with that relaxation. See what you notice.

Once you can notice where the subjective center of the self is, you can let it relax. When a hindrance arises, rather than relax that hindrance, relax the self that experiences the hindrance.

This has the same effect as relaxing the tension in a hindrance. Without a self, there are no hindrances — just a flow of phenomena. It is tension that divides the flow of experience into categories of "self" and "other."

## Lobha, Dosa, and Moha

If we are not able to relax the barrier between Self and Other, then Other begets three children: triplets. They have been given different names:

The Three Poisons

Attraction, Aversion, Confusion

Liking, Disliking, Ignorance

Lust, Hatred, Delusion

Lobha, Dosa, Moha (*Pāli*)

I like the *Pāli* terms because they imply a greater range than any English equivalent. *Lobha* includes everything from the craving of a drug addict to the subtle daydream of a vacation. *Dosa* includes everything from rage to sullenness. *Moha* includes willful ignorance and innocent misguidedness or bad information.

I also like them because they sound like Larry, Curley, Moe: the Three Stooges. They get into trouble, suffer a lot, and yet we can imagine they have innocent hearts. All hindrances are like this – innocent and confused.

# The Big Five

If we don't relax the tension in them, lobha, dosa, and moha soon beget five children. These are the five hindrances or five *nīvaraṇa*:

Desire: The urge to move toward something or to draw it to us.

Aversion: The urge to get away from something or to drive it off.

Restlessness: More energy than we can manage.

Sloth and torpor: Too little energy to stay aware, wisely engaged, and motivated.

Doubt: Including doubt in ourselves, doubt in the practice, and doubt in the form of an inner critic.

I call them "the big five hindrances" because they are mentioned as a group throughout the Buddha's talks.

# Going Forth and Multiplying

If we don't relax the tension in these five, they go forth and multiply. They beget multitudes. And we may get overwhelmed.

In the next chapter we'll look in detail at eleven hindrances the Buddha described in one of his talks. But there are many more.

For now I'd like to summarize this chapter by emphasizing that the problem with hindrances is not the hindrances themselves — the veils or coverings that conceal or distort our experience. It is our attitude toward them that can give us trouble.

This story that captures a wise attitude in a simple phrase.

*Once there was a monk who lived in a little hut just outside a small fishing village.*

*One day, a young, unmarried woman in the village got pregnant. The people were upset and demanded to know who the father was. She loved the young man and didn't want to get him into trouble, so she said the father was the monk living just outside of town.*

*When her child was born, a delegation of elders gathered up the child, marched to the monk's dwelling, and rapped on his door. He opened the door and looked at them with a quiet smile.*

*They frowned and said, "Here. This is your child," and handed it to him.*

*"Ah so," he said, bowing slightly. They turned and marched away.*

*Fifteen years later the mother became ill. She knew she was dying. She didn't want to have that terrible lie on her conscience. So she confessed the truth.*

*Shortly thereafter, a delegation of elders walked quietly to the monk's cabin, knocked softly on the door, and stood contritely. The monk opened the door and looked at them with a quiet smile. Behind him was a teenager with sparkly eyes. The elders said, "We are so sorry. We know this child is not your responsibility. We have come to relieve you of this burden."*

*The monk replied, "Ah so."*

If this were a story about living in the world, then the next day after the elders left the baby and quieted down, the monk would have walked into town to discuss with them what was going on. Living in the world, there are often things to be done in response to events.

But this is a story about meditation. Sitting in meditation, there is rarely anything to be done outwardly. We view the disturbance, the fascination, the fear, the hindrance with a gentle "Ah so."

It's a simple acknowledgement of what is true in the moment: "Here is a distortion. Ah so."

Given the stresses in our lives, it is no surprise that desire, aversion, restlessness, sloth, torpor, doubt, and many other things arise when we meditate. If we fully understood them, we wouldn't rail against them. We'd just say, "Of course," or "No big surprise this arose," or "Ah so."

So when distractions grab our attention, we can greet them with, "Ah so." In it is Recognition and Release. It's Relaxed. It has a quiet smile (Re-Smile). And it gently Returns to radiating mettā.

> *To study the way is to study the self.*
> *To study the self is to lose the self.*
> *To lose the self is to be enlightened by all things.*
> *To be enlightened by all things*
> *Is to remove the barrier between self and other.*

– Dōgen (13<sup>th</sup> century Zen monk)

# 3

# Dancing with the Demons

Understanding that hindrances can be a blessing is helpful, but often it's not enough. We have to actually engage them — dance with the demons, as it were — to truly learn and deepen. So let's shift from the last chapter's overview of hindrances to examining the nitty-gritty of specific hindrances and how we might dance with them with more kindness and wisdom.

In the "Upakkilesa Sutta" (*Majjhima Nikāya* 128), the Buddha mentions 11 hindrances. "Upakkilesa" is usually translated as "imperfections," "obscurations," "defilements" or "mental impurities." It really means hindrances or mental nuisances that pull our attention away from our chosen object of meditation.

In verse 7 of the sutta, the Buddha leaves a fractious schism in the capital city of Kosambi and wanders over to the Eastern Bamboo Park where he meets his first cousin, the monk Anuruddha. Anuruddha is living peacefully with two other monks, Nandiya and Kimbila. Fresh out of the brouhaha in Kosambi, he asks Anuruddha how they live in such concord.

Anuruddha says they are kind to one another; that each places the others' needs before his own; that they look out for each other, share the chores, and so forth. He says, "We are different in body, but one in mind. ...blending like milk and water and viewing each other with kindly eyes" (verse 12). They play well together. And they meditate together.

# Jhāna

The Buddha picks up this reference to meditation:

15. *"Good, good, Anuruddha... Have you attained any superhuman states, a distinction in knowledge and vision worthy of the noble ones, a comfortable abiding?"*

*"Venerable sir, as we abide here diligent, ardent, and resolute, we perceive both light and a vision of forms. Soon afterwards the light and the vision of forms disappear, but we have not discovered the cause for that."*

"Superhuman states" doesn't mean superpowers. The term "super" just means "above the norm." It means *jhāna* or "higher stage of meditation." "Comfortable abiding" means "equanimity." The Buddha is asking if they enter jhānas and rest stably there.

Anuruddha replies that they perceive "light and a vision of forms." "Light" means a feeling of radiance. "Vision of forms" refers to staying with the object of meditation or mindfulness.

In other words, they start off meditating well. The mind-heart becomes light and luminous. Their attention stays on the object of meditation comfortably. But soon it all collapses, and they don't know why.

We all know that place: the good sitting that gets overrun by hindrances. We Six-R, but the hindrances persist. Perhaps we're mystified at what's going on.

The Buddha says:

16. *"You should discover the cause for that, Anuruddha. Before my enlightenment, while I was still only an unenlightened Bodhisattva, I too perceived both radiance and the object of meditation. Soon afterwards the radiance and mindfulness disappeared. I thought: 'What is the cause and condition why have the radiance and mindfulness have disappeared?' Then I considered thus: 'Doubt arose in me, and because of the doubt my stability of mind fell away; when my collectedness fell away, the radiance and mindfulness disappeared. I shall so act that doubt will not arise in me again.'*

Let's unpack this.

As I said earlier, when a hindrance hijacks our attention, the first thing we do is Six-R. Sometimes after Six-R'ing once or a number of times, the hindrance fades. And sometimes the hindrance returns again and again with the same strength.

The Buddha says, "You ought to ask why that's persisting." To do this, simply ask, "What's going on?" or "Am I missing something?" Then let go of the question and go back to meditating. The question invites the mind-heart to pay closer attention.

The Buddha goes on to say that back in the old days before he was awakened, sometimes when he asked that question, he realized that doubt was a problem.

Perhaps doubt was Anuruddha's original hindrance. Or perhaps his original hindrance was something else — maybe restlessness. But as the restlessness persisted, he began to doubt the practice, doubt his ability to meditate productively, or doubt the Dhamma.

In other words, he had an unwholesome response to an unwholesome state: a hindrance attack. Hindrances draw other hindrances. They like to run around in gangs.

If this is the case, it helps to let the original hindrance run off and do what it wants while we attend to the doubt, release it, relax any tension, smile, and return to our object of meditation.

As we relax the tightness in the doubt, the doubt will gradually subside. Along with that, the original hindrance (restlessness) begins to run out of gas.

Verse 17 is the same as 16 except for a key term. He speaks of inattention rather than doubt: "...*Then I considered thus: **inattention** arose in me, and because of the **inattention** my stability of mind fell away...*" (bold added). Other verses follow suit with different key terms until he has mentioned 11 hindrances.

I'd like to look at each of these from verse 16 to 26, starting with the key term and what it means. Then I'll suggest how to relate to it with kindness and wisdom when the Six Rs themselves don't seem to be enough.

# Doubt

As I mentioned, the first specific hindrance the Buddha refers to is doubt — a loss of confidence or loss of faith in oneself or the practice. Nothing is wrong with a healthy skepticism if it motivates us to look more carefully into what's going on or encourages us to investigate our experience more openly. The doubt the Buddha is concerned about is a cynical closing of the mind and heart — a turning away out of a negative bias.

One antidote for this doubt is curiosity — taking more interest in our experience. Reflecting on our motivations may also help. Curiosity and investigation are awakening factors or qualities that can bring us out of the dead end of overbearing doubt.

# Inattention

In verse 17, the Buddha moves on to a second hindrance called "inattention" or "nonattention." This means having more interest in something other than meditation while we're meditating. Earlier I mentioned wanting to develop zingers to win an argument, and designing a desk lamp while on retreat. I can blame the fight or the desk lamp for hindering my progress, but they were a problem only because I was more interested in them than meditation. These are examples of "inattention" or "non-attention."

As with doubt, antidotes for inattention include taking more genuine interest in the object of meditation and reflecting on our underlying motivation. It doesn't help to criticize ourselves for having mixed motivations. But it does help to honestly and kindly acknowledge what is going on. Wholesome recognition of unwholesome qualities brings more wholesomeness into the mind-heart.

# Sloth and Torpor

Torpor is dull or sleepy awareness — the mind can feel foggy. Sloth is a loss of motivation. Often sloth and torpor arise together, as in "Ho hum. My mind is dull. I'll Six-R in a few minutes."

Anything that perks up the mind or motivation can help. Energy, joy, and investigation are awakening factors that bring more energy. Sometimes it's enough to just invite more energy into the system — not pushing or grasping but just opening to it. Smiling is one of many ways to invite some joy. Investigation might include looking more closely at what we're actually experiencing. For example, when I feel groggy, I sometimes notice a dull ache in the back of my head and thick, misty awareness. Taking more interest in seeing the sensations we're calling "grogginess" or "dullness" can bring clarity and make them seem simpler.

If this doesn't help the mind lighten, there are other strategies. Taking a few deep breaths brings more oxygen into the body and increases its energy. Meditating with the eyes open or while standing up brings more alertness. Meditating outside can freshen the system. Shifting into walking meditation can help the blood circulate and raise energy levels. Walking backwards can sharpen attention.

If these kinds of strategies fail, ask "Am I a bit sleep deprived?" The mind and body are truly interdependent. If our physical energy is just too tired, the best thing may be to take a nap and start again when we're fresher.

# Fear

In verse 19, the Buddha talks about fear. Fear is a signal that something is threatening the integrity of our organism. Fear tries to protect us — we can be grateful for this. However, usually we're not grateful because it's...well...frightening.

Fear comes in many varieties: some are real and immediate; some are real but loom in the future or drift like ghosts from the past; and some are imaginary. Nevertheless, the feeling itself can be quite compelling. When the feeling is too enthusiastic or unwise, it can make meditation and life miserable for no good purpose. So I'd like to spend a little extra time with this hindrance to sort out ways to engage fear wisely and compassionately.

### Real and Immediate Fear

The simplest fear is about threats that are real and immediate. For example, we can't remember if we turned the stove off. With this kind of fear, we needn't bother to Six-R. It's best to take care of the threat: get up and check the stove.

When we return to meditation, the fear may linger. It can take a while to metabolize the hormones that stimulate fear sensations. If so, we can simply observe those sensations and Six-R them.

### Real and Looming Fear

Another type of fear is real but looms in the future: we're worried about an upcoming job review; we wonder if a friend was offended by an off-hand comment we made; or we're concerned about what may show up in the blood tests we just sent to the lab.

We might ask, "Is there something wise to do about it now?" or conversely, "Would I be better off meditating now and tending to it later?" The questions aren't meant to start a mental debate. They are used to direct awareness from the thought content to deeper intuitive wisdom.

If it is wiser to meditate now, this doesn't mean the thinking will stop. Evolution has bred the mind to figure out solutions to dangers. We need not beat ourselves up or blame the mind up for trying to do its job. However, we don't want to indulge the thinking either. The mind can make up endless stories to justify what it feels. It's not helpful.

Rather than trying to stop the thinking or indulging it, we just notice the worry and relax into it. We drop the storyline without trying to expel it. This feels like letting it go outside and run around on its own while we bring awareness back to the present moment. How does the mind-heart feel? What are its textures, its moods, its tensions? We let tightness soften.

As the tensions soften, the mind will gradually unwind itself. Meanwhile, we aren't feeding the thinking by a big deal of it. Patience helps.

## Nebulous and Unclear Fear

With another variety of fear, the source of the threat is less clear. Like Jacob waking in the night, we feel anxiousness or urgency without knowing what it's about. The mind quickly starts looking for culprits. In our world and in our lives, lots of candidates are willing to step into the spotlight.

Before we assign a culprit, it's best to Six-R the sensations themselves. It's best to see if we can sit openly with the feelings rather than jump up and blame a villain for them.

Sooner or later most of us meet a demon in the night — a fear that is compelling but difficult to see clearly. A common one is the growing realization that the ego-mind is not in charge. We don't have the control we thought we had. Something else is piloting the plane. We are only navigators watching where the plane goes and advising the pilot. But we don't have the flight controls.

If we had a stressful day, it is likely to show up in our meditation practice whether we like it or not. Our lives are governed by natural, impersonal laws that don't care about our preferences.

Other demons are old feeling tones from a long time ago. They arise out of our history and conditioning.

For example, I grew up in a family with a flat emotional expression. I thought placidness was normal and that the feelings swirling through me were defects. Attempts to stifle them contributed to a diffuse, chronic, low-grade depression. I was in my late 20s before I realized there was more to life than shades of grey.

It took me a dozen years of therapy, bodywork, and meditation to finally break the clinical depression.

Some years later I went to Thailand to learn meditation from Ajahn Tong, a Thai forest master. Every week or two he asked me to meditate around the clock without sleeping for three or four days at a stretch. As the mind became more and more peaceful, a pervasive sense of aloneness emerged.

It didn't help that 95 percent of the people around me didn't speak English and that my family was on the far side of the planet. But it didn't feel like an adult loneliness. I felt abandoned and helpless, like a baby left alone in a cold darkness.

These feelings were the hidden origins of the clinical depression I had broken 15 years earlier. These were the subtle roots deep inside. It was quietly overwhelming.

We all have our stories. Some stories are worse than mine. Some are not as difficult. But this side of enlightenment we all have imbalances. As the mind quiets down in deep meditation, these soft, distant voices may be heard for the first time in years.

They are the demons in the night that Jacob felt. How do we relate to them?

I spoke to a monk about my predicament. He smiled empathetically and said, "Yes, I once touched such a place. It was so terrible that I ran out of my *kuti* (meditation hut) and across the rice field to get away. But the feelings traveled with me. So I went back to my *kuti* to meditate. There was no escape. I had to face them sooner or later. Why not face them now?"

Encouraged by his words, I went back to my *kuti* to meditate. Rather than run from the loneliness, I tried to open to it with kindness and compassion. Gradually, with time and many ups and downs, the ancient loneliness that had gripped my heart began to loosen.

How this works is described in more detail later (p. 51). Briefly it looks like this:

Underneath fear is hurt. It may be the hurt of abuse or abandonment or failure. Suffering has many varieties. But beneath fear always lies hurt or the anticipation of hurt.

Under hurt is tenderness. Without sensitivity, we wouldn't hurt.

Beneath the tenderness is spaciousness. Without openness, there would be no tenderness.

The spaciousness is the equanimity and quiet joy we seek. It's the demon's blessing — something beneficial hidden beneath the hurt. We can't find spaciousness, equanimity, or joy by running from the fear or hurt, or numbing out the tenderness.

The enveloping peacefulness won't jump up and down and wave its arms to get attention. That's not its nature. It is quiet and patient.

We can only soften through the layers of fear, hurt, and tenderness to find that immeasurable peace that has been waiting quietly all the time.

It's up to us to find the wisdom and courage to relax through the disturbances to find what's always been here.

Many years later, while leading meditation retreats, I saw different versions of this process in other yogis. One might come to me and say, "Horrible images seep into my meditation: dark, bloody, gut wrenching. I feel like I'm going crazy. How can I get rid of them? I don't want them."

If I'm confident in their basic emotional stability, I say, "What you want is not relevant. The only thing that's relevant is what's true. And the truth is these images and feelings are arising.

"I don't think the meditation is creating them. It's just revealing them. They've been hiding. Your awareness is getting strong enough to see into dark shadows."

At this point, I like to quote Maurice Sendak's children's story: "And when he came to the place where the wild things are, they roared their terrible roars and gnashed their terrible teeth and rolled their terrible eyes and showed their terrible claws till Max said, 'Be still' and tamed them with the magic trick of staring into all their yellow eyes without blinking once."[6]

Then I suggest to the yogi, "If you feel up to it, you can go back into meditation and call the fear's bluff. You can look into its yellow

---

[6] Maurice Sendak. *Where the Wild Things Are,* Harper & Row, 1963

eyes and say, 'Thank you for showing me that deep holding. I'm not going to fight you. I'm not going to run anymore. So go ahead and do your worst.' Then open your heart and relax as best you can into the fear. Surrender into it and see what happens.

"Don't pay attention to what your mind says about the fear. What it says is not helpful or relevant. Just open to the preverbal sensations of the fear itself and let them flow through you. Fear will generate lots of stories to justify itself. You can ignore those and just soften into the feeling itself.

"See what happens."

You don't have to do this all at once. You can open bit by bit, little by little. As you get your sea legs in these larger energies, you'll naturally relax and open more and more.

This process may take you through the fear, hurt, and tenderness into the great luminous spaciousness that is the demon-angel's blessing that's within the fear or hurt.

So far, no yogi has gone crazy. And some have felt a transformative relief. Most fear is just resistance to fear. As we open to what's here, the mind-heart's natural luminosity emerges out of the dark clouds.

This is what happened to me in Southeast Asia. The Doug who came home from Thailand was not the Doug who went there. I still have plenty of neuroses. But when I came back, I knew freedom was tangible, and closer than I'd imagined.

# Elation

The next hindrance the Buddha describes is elation. Some translate the term as "jubilation" or "excitement." Basically, it means having too much energy. The energy may feel very good, but we are happy to the point of wanting to think about it or describe it to others. We like it and hold onto it.

These days as my meditation settles in, my body often chuckles as it relaxes. The chuckle is involuntary. And it's not a problem. It becomes a problem only if I obsess about it.

The first remedy for elation is to Six-R. Let go of the storyline. Then let the good feeling soak into your bones.

It also helps to intentionally open to some of the quieter awakening factors: equanimity, tranquility, and investigation. They can help balance the mind-heart.

## Staleness

In verse 21, the Buddha talks about inertia or inaction as a hindrance. Perhaps it's more helpful to think of this hindrance as staleness. It's a sort of "ho hum" as the dull mind goes through the motions of meditation without real interest. It's a form of boredom.

One remedy is to take more interest in the meditation — really see what's going on. Another is to take a break. On longer retreats, my teacher Bhante Vimalaraṁsi, would come pick me up every week or two to take me and a few other yogis out of the meditation center for the day. We'd drive through the Missouri Ozarks and visit deep hot springs or historic sites — something to break up the routine.

The next day when I went back to meditation practice, the mind felt refreshed and ready to go.

Staleness can seem a lot like sloth and torpor. And it is somewhat. These hindrances are not completely separate phenomena.

However, staleness is something that is more likely to occur when we've been meditating so much that the mind has drifted into inertia. We're doing the practice okay, but progress has slowed down and we've lost the sense of freshness.

Taking a break from the routine or just going off and having some fun may do the trick.

# Excessive Effort

The next hindrance is excessive effort. Excessive effort leads to excessive energy. This often comes from a desire to make something happen or to push something away. We are putting more into controlling the experience than into observing it. The most common mistake Western yogis make is trying too hard.

I find it helpful to think of myself less as meditation student and more as a field naturalist. Good naturalists are more interested in quietly seeing what the animals do than in shaping animals' behavior. Skillful meditators are more interested in seeing what their mind does than in trying to shape their experience. They gently remind themselves, "What happens doesn't matter. Just observe." This helps us let go of the subtle pushing.

Sometimes the excessive effort can creep up so slowly that we don't notice.

During the first few years of my meditation training, I made progress. It felt good. Then an inner swirling showed up on longer retreats. I felt spun around and around. I even had vertigo.

To get rid of the feeling, I tried to hold on to the sensation of the breath to steady myself. But that made the swirling worse. In fact, everything I did made it worse except distracting myself with wandering thoughts. My progress was coming to a halt.

After about a year of this (I'm a slow learner) I wondered what would happen if, rather than struggle against the whirlwind, I surrendered into it. What if I just let it take me for a ride? I wasn't confident it would help. It would be like standing on the deck of a ship in a storm and letting go of the railing. But everything else had failed. Surrendering was the only other option I could think of.

So I relaxed into the storm. Almost immediately, it slowed. That excited me. The excitement started the whirling again. But I was beginning to learn that relaxing into the sensation allowed the storm to unwind.

This is similar to relaxing into fear. Relaxing into fear allows it to spread out and get bigger and bigger. As the fear grows, it thins out. Eventually it dissolves like a mist evaporating in the morning sun.

Sayadaw U Tejaniya asks, "What do meditation, going to sleep, and going to the toilet have in common?" The answer is: they all work better if we don't try too hard.

# Weak Effort

The opposite of excessive effort is too little effort. This is less common in the West and perhaps more common in cultures that are more devotional in temperament. However, I do see it here.

This hindrance is similar to sloth and torpor. When we're physically tired, the mind may grow dull through lack of effort. However, the solution for weak effort is simply developing more interest in the object of meditation. We can also bring in some of the energizing awakening factors: energy, joy, and curiosity.

*One evening on retreat, I couldn't sleep. My mind was just too alert. So I got up to meditate. I ended up meditating through most of the night.*

*At 5:30, I was supposed to come to a group sitting in which we recited the refuges and precepts. I was very tired from lack of sleep. The 5:30 meditation period officially ran until breakfast time at 7:00.*

*I knew that after reciting the refuges and precepts, it was perfectly fine for me to go back to my* kuti *and sleep. But something in my German blood or my Taurus personality kicked in. I was determined to sit still until 7:00 even if I was on the edge of falling asleep.*

*Rather than force myself to sit there, I decided to see what would happen if I invited joy into my sitting. I wasn't forcing it, just inviting it.*

*My energy came up just fine, and I had a clear and still meditation with a fair amount of joy. It felt balanced.*

*After breakfast, I went back to my* kuti *and slept for two hours.*

The moral of this story is to not try harder when we're tired. It's never to try harder. But if the effort is weak, bringing in more energy can bring the mind into balance. If we can bring in more energy or curiosity or joy, they may enliven our system.

And if they don't, then a nap is good.

# Longing

In verse 24, the Buddha talks about longing. Longing is soft and sweet desire. Often we long for something wholesome, such as equanimity, compassion, ease, heart, or even nibbāna. Nothing is wrong with the objects of these desires.

But the desire itself can be a problem. The trick is to take our attention off the longing for a vacation, a good sitting, an open heart, or whatever. Rather, let the attention come to the longing itself. See it as clearly as we can. And Six-R to return to the primary object of meditation — sending out uplifted qualities.

This process allows the longing to expend itself without us getting entangled in it.

# Variety of Perceptions

In verse 25, the Buddha talks about a variety of perceptions. The key word is often translated as "perception of diversity." But the diversity is not the problem. The problem is that the mind keeps moving from one thing to another.

This hindrance may show up as the desire to have a different spiritual friend, or the desire to do several different kinds of practices at once, or the urge to think about Buddhist concepts or find something more entertaining. Sometimes the mind is a little bored and looks for amusement. This is a form of restlessness — a dull expression of too much energy.

The solution is to relax and Six-R the subtle restlessness.

Other times the mind is just following its natural inclinations. So let's look more closely at these inclinations.

Evolution bred curiosity into the human brain. Our prehuman ancestors were scavengers. To survive, they needed a wide knowledge of where food and dangers were in the environment. Those with a natural curiosity were better at mapping the world around them. They were more likely to survive long enough to pass on their inclinations.

One sign of curiosity is youthful play. The young of intelligent species enjoy imagining different scenarios and acting them out. The human brain enjoys thinking. It's part of its design.

We have the nature of scavengers. When the mind jumps around from topic to topic, elaborates on stories, imagines different possibilities, envisions various situations, it's just doing its job. It's not helpful to fight this fundamental property of the human organism.

However, having a mind that jumps around is not conducive to peace, wisdom, and compassion.

We have seen a simple solution with other hindrances. If the mind is busy thinking, we can let go of the thoughts and stories and notice how the thinking feels. If the awareness feels tense, then relax and Six-R. However, if the mind genuinely feels good — if it's enjoying the variety — we don't have to stop it. Rather, we can shift awareness from the thought content to the enjoyment itself. If it's a good feeling, it's a wholesome quality. We don't need to get rid of it. Instead we can let it soak into our bones.

If the mind is grasping for good qualities, the grasping is a hindrance to be relaxed. But if good qualities are present, they are uplifted feelings that can be savored. They're what the mind-heart wants, and it is wise and helpful to let them soak in.

As this happens, the mind-heart will naturally soften and expand. The thought content will gently dissolve.

## Excessive Meditation on Forms

The last hindrance the Buddha mentions in this sutta is called "excessive meditation on forms." This hindrance is in the same family as excessive energy and excessive effort.

Excessive meditation on forms is too much seriousness. The awakened mind is light, clear, uplifted, and peaceful. Sometimes we can get too serious. This may cause the practice to get thick and heavy.

The simplest solution is to just see the seriousness and smile. This is a smiling practice. The lighter the mind, the clearer it becomes.

We can also shift our attention from the meditation object that we are taking seriously and toward the serious attitude itself. Bringing clear awareness to the seriousness helps it lighten up.

It feels like taking our foot off the gas. We trust that things will arise in their own time. We don't push the river. We cannot hurry the mind-heart's natural unfolding. But by taking it too seriously, we can slow it down.

# Attitude

We tend to view hindrances as if they were demons in the dark, party poopers, or mangy dogs with muddy feet. We tend to view them with aversion, tightness, confusion, or aggression.

In wisdom practices there are no hindrances as such. In one-pointed practice, hindrances take us off our one point. In wisdom practice, whatever arises is just fine if we can see it clearly and impersonally.

*The bottom line is: be aware of your attitude toward your experience.* If the attitude is unwelcoming, see it kindly. Release it, relax, and smile. When we can receive a powerful demon with the same openness as a beloved friend, then we are free.

Ah so.

# 4

# Kindness and a Patient Heart

The poet Naomi Shihab Nye writes:

*Wandering around the Albuquerque Airport Terminal, after learning my flight had been delayed four hours, I heard an announcement: "If anyone in the vicinity of Gate A-4 understands any Arabic, please come to the gate immediately."*

*Well — one pauses these days. Gate A-4 was my own gate. I went there.*

*An older woman in full traditional Palestinian embroidered dress, just like my grandma wore, was crumpled to the floor, wailing loudly. "Help," said the flight service person. "Talk to her. What is her problem? We told her the flight was going to be late and she did this."*

*I stooped to put my arm around the woman and spoke to her haltingly. "Shu-dow-a, Shu-bid-uck Habibti? Stani schway, Min fadlick, Shu-bit-se-wee?" The minute she heard any words she knew, however poorly used, she stopped crying. She thought the flight had been canceled entirely. She needed to be in El Paso for major medical treatment the next day. I said, "No, we're fine, you'll get there, just later. Who is picking you up? Let's call him."*

*We called her son, and I spoke with him in English. I told him I would stay with his mother till we got on the plane and would ride next to her — Southwest. She talked to him. Then we called her other sons just for the fun of it. Then we called my dad and he and she spoke for a while in Arabic and found out of course they had ten shared friends. Then I thought just for the heck of it why not call some Palestinian poets I know and let them chat with her? This all took up about two hours.*

*She was laughing a lot by then. Telling about her life, patting my knee, answering questions. She had pulled a sack of homemade mamool cookies — little powdered sugar crumbly mounds stuffed with dates and nuts — out of her bag — and was offering them to all the women at the gate. To my amazement, not a single woman declined one. It was like a sacrament. The traveler from Argentina, the mom from California, the lovely woman from Laredo — we were all covered with the same powdered sugar. And smiling. There is no better cookie.*

*And then the airline broke out free beverages from huge coolers and two little girls from our flight ran around serving us all apple juice and they were covered with powdered sugar, too. And I noticed my new best friend — by now we were holding hands — had a potted plant poking out of her bag, some medicinal thing, with green furry leaves. Such an old country tradition. Always carry a plant. Always stay rooted to somewhere.*

*And I looked around that gate of late and weary ones and I thought, This is the world I want to live in. The shared world. Not a single person in that gate — once the crying of confusion stopped — seemed apprehensive about any other person. They took the cookies. I wanted to hug all those other women, too.*

*This can still happen anywhere. Not everything is lost.*

– Naomi Shihab Nye[7]

Kindness is near and dear to the heart of Buddhism. The Buddha wasn't interested in other worlds or metaphysical pronouncements. He saw such views as distractions from his more earthy intentions: relieving suffering and cultivating well-being. Part of his path to freedom from suffering was cultivating the four so-called *Brahmavihāras* or "heavenly abodes." These wholesome qualities are *mettā, karuṇā, muditā, and upekkhā* — kindness, compassion, joy, and equanimity.

The *Pāli* word *mettā* is usually translated as "loving kindness." The root of mettā might be better translated as "friend." Mettā is friendliness toward all. True kindness is not highfalutin. It's ordinary, unpresumptuous friendliness, like the way Naomi Shihab

---

[7] "Gate A-4" from *Honey Bee: Poems & Short Prose*, (Greenwillow Books, 2008).

Nye cared for the older Palestinian woman, the way the woman shared *mamool*, and the way everyone at Gate A-4 began to smile.

I've studied Buddhist practice for over 40 years. From this I've learned a lot about kindness and friendliness. Buddhism is probably better known for mindfulness, insight, and wisdom. But wisdom without kindness is not wise. And kindness without wisdom is not kind. Friendliness, wisdom, and peace are intertwined. They are different ways of looking at the same wholesome quality.

The last three *Brahmavihāras* flow naturally from simple kindness. If we are with someone whose levels of suffering and well-being are about the same as ours, the outflowing of the heart feels like kindness. If they are suffering more than us, the same flow of kindness feels like compassion. If they are in better shape than us, the flow of kindness feels like joy. If we can do nothing about their suffering, the same flow feels like equanimity. Mettā, or gentle kindness, is the root of all of the *Brahmavihāras*.

So I'd like to explore how to cultivate kindness and the patient heart.

# Tenderness and Spaciousness

The model for moving from hurt to tenderness to spaciousness (which was briefly introduced on p. 40) looks like this:

We all experience *dukkha:* suffering, hurt, pain, angst, discouragement, fear, and bummers. Is there anyone who has never suffered?

The Buddha never said, "life is suffering," or "life is a bummer." He only said that "life has bummers" — along with love, contentment, peace, and other things. Dukkha is part of the mix.

When we look gently and openly beneath our suffering, we notice tenderness. Without tenderness we wouldn't hurt.

When we look gently and openly beneath tenderness, we notice spaciousness. Without this openness, we'd feel numb rather than tender.

On the spiritual path, many of us seek spaciousness and the clarity and wisdom that come with it. To find these we may try to fight off pain, push aside hurt, or distract ourselves from upset. We may try to make an end-run around discomfort.

But it doesn't work in the long run. When we turn away from discomfort, we also turn away from the natural tenderness and kindness beneath.

It's more effective to face toward the discomfort and relax into it. We can gently ignore our stories and justifications and soften until we feel the tenderness. We can continue to relax into the tenderness until we sense the simple well-being waiting to be noticed. Then we can savor the well-being and let it soak into our bones.

This is the path to kindness I've learned from the Buddha: turning toward, relaxing into, and savoring.

# Wired In

To say this differently, kindness is inherent in us humans. The tendency is wired into us. It's embedded deep in our neural circuitry. It swept through those people at Gate 4-A because it is infectious. It's in our nature to be kind.

If you think this sounds naïve, I don't blame you. We live in polarized times. Ill will flows from some of the most powerful people in the world. Mean-spiritedness can drown out friendliness. Hurry and worry, stress and fear, greed and me-ism can push our kinder inclinations under a rock.

Turning toward, relaxing into, and savoring are simple. But they aren't easy. So I'd like to explore these three practices.

# Three Essential Practices

The three essential practices have been passed down to us as "The Four Noble Truths." But if we read how the Buddha actually described them, it's clear they aren't declarations of capital "T" truths. They are simple observations of life. And each observation has a practice associated with it. They are meditation instructions that are pithy and effective enough to be used in daily life.

The Buddha first introduced the four truths in his first talk with the five ascetics in the deer park in Sarnath. That talk is now called the "Dhammacakkappavattana Sutta: Setting the Wheel of Dhamma in Motion" (*Saṃyutta Nikāya* 56.11). An article on my website called "Turning Toward"[8] goes through the Buddha's words line by line showing how the four truths are actually these three essential practices. The fourth truth is an eightfold checklist of things we can do to fine-tune our practice. But the first three are the essence of the practices.

For now, I want to just focus on the first three observations and practices.

# Turning Toward

The first practice is called "fully understanding suffering." The text (*Saṃyutta Nikāya* 56.11) reads:

> *"Now this, monks, is the noble truth of suffering: birth is suffering, aging is suffering, illness is suffering, death is suffering; sorrow, pain, lamentations, grief, and despair are suffering; association with what is displeasing is suffering; separation from what is pleasing is suffering; not to get what one wants is suffering; in brief, the five aggregates affected by clinging are suffering...*
>
> *"This is the noble truth of suffering": thus, monks, in regard to things unheard before, there arose in me vision, knowledge, wisdom, true knowledge, and light.*
>
> *"This noble truth of suffering is to be fully understood": thus, monks, in regard to things unheard before, there arose in me vision, knowledge, wisdom, true knowledge, and light.*
>
> *"This noble truth of suffering has been fully understood": thus, monks, in regard to things unheard before, there arose in me vision, knowledge, wisdom, true knowledge, and light.*[9]

---

[8] https://www.dougkraft.com/?p=TurningToward
[9] These passages were rendered from translations by Bhikkhu Bodhi and Thanissaro Bhikkhu.

The repetition in the text indicate that it's been stylized to aid memorization and oral transmission. Much of text was not written down until centuries after the Buddha died.

Parts of the passage may sound like braggadocio. This tone probably crept into the text over the years out of reverence for the Buddha and the desire to impress listeners and win converts. I doubt the Buddha actually bragged.

The first line lists various experiences the Buddha considered to be suffering. We'll come back to this list in the next chapter (p. 71) when we look more closely at the nature of experience itself. For now it's enough to note that the list was not meant to define suffering but to give examples of it.

The essence of the passage is repeated three times, as is common in oral transmission. In this case he says, (1) there is suffering, (2) suffering is to be understood, and (3) suffering has been understood by me. Saying he understood suffering could be interpreted as bragging or as trying to inspire them by implying, "If you do the same, you'll achieve what I have achieved." I doubt he was bragging.

To fully understand someone, we have to do more than diagnose them. We have to know the person empathetically and intimately. We have to know how they tick, what motivates them, how they see the world, what frightens them, what they aspire to. To fully understand ourselves, we need the same kind of empathy for ourselves.

Similarly, the Buddha said that to lead fulfilling lives we must fully understand the nature of suffering, dissatisfaction, and bummers. Arms-length analysis is not enough. We have to know how bummers feel, how they arise, how they move, how they pass away. It's not helpful to get wrapped up in the stories and thoughts about the bummers. But it helps to see their underlying processes.

We'll never find this deep understanding if we're turning away or trying to shield ourselves from discomfort. We must experience it intimately without resistance, beginning with turning toward it. Here's a metaphor:

*I lived in Houston for my first 16 years. Once or twice a week in the hot summers, my siblings and I tumbled into our family's blue-and-white Chevy station wagon, and our mother drove us to Galveston so we could play in the Gulf of Mexico.*

*Houston is 60 miles from Galveston and 60 feet above sea level. The land slopes downward at a rate of one foot per mile: about as flat as one can imagine. The Gulf floor is only a little steeper. We could wade out several hundred feet and only be waist deep.*

*When big waves came, trying to escape them was futile. Running through the water was exhausting, and the shore was too far. If we tried to get away, the waves caught us from behind and knocked us flat.*

*So we planted our feet and braced as the waves crashed upon us. This worked for the small waves. But water is heavy. Big waves outweighed us ten to one. We got knocked over.*

*Finally we learned that the best way to greet a wave was to surrender into it. When the wave was really big, we'd relax and dive into it.*

*As scary and frothy as the waves seemed when they roared toward us, if we relaxed into them, the surf passed over us and left us in the essence of the wave: sea water, plain old sea water. Not so bad.*

*Then our natural buoyancy brought us to the surface so that we floated in that little trough of peace between the waves.*

If we try to run from discomfort, it's likely to catch us from behind and knock us flat. If we brace against the discomfort, we get worn down quickly. If we try to push discomfort below the waves like a beach ball, when we tire or relax it pops back up in our faces.

The Buddha said, "Face discomfort openly until you know how it works. You must fully understand."

Our lives get washed over with many kinds of good and bad waves: love for our kids, worry about our kids, falling in love, relationship ruffles, financial strain, good fortune, illness, health, brouhahas, embarrassments, accomplishments, satisfaction, political inanity, and more.

When we engage life's difficulties openly, we see how all these waves arise and pass. But we don't have to be passive. Sometimes there are important actions to be taken. However, before we act it's helpful to cultivate a little peace and kindness so that our actions are more likely to be born of wisdom.

# Relaxing Into

When we turn toward and open up to life's difficult waves in this way, we come to see that the experience of suffering is rooted in tension. This brings us to the second of the three practices. I call it "relaxing into." The text reads:

> *This, monks, is the noble truth of the origin of suffering: the craving which leads to further becoming — accompanied by delight and passion, relishing now here and now there; that is, craving for sensual pleasures, craving for becoming, craving for non-becoming...*

> *"This is the noble truth of the origin of suffering": thus, monks, in regard to things unheard before, there arose in me vision, knowledge, wisdom, true knowledge, and light.*

> *"This noble truth of the origin of suffering is to be abandoned": thus, monks, in regard to things unheard before, there arose in me vision, knowledge, wisdom, true knowledge, and light.*

> *"This noble truth of the origin of suffering has been abandoned": thus, monks, in regard to things unheard before, there arose in me vision, knowledge, wisdom, true knowledge, and light.*

In short the Buddha is saying the origin of suffering is *taṇhā*, a Pāli term translated here as craving. He elaborates by saying (1) suffering has its origins in taṇhā, (2) suffering is to be abandoned, and (3) suffering has been abandoned by me. If you do the same thing, you'll get what I have gotten.

# Taṇhā

Taṇhā is an instinctual tightening that usually arises without forethought or conscious intention. When we are about to step off the sidewalk and notice a car coming our way, the body tightens. It's a survival reflex that energizes us to deal with a potential threat. We don't think about it, contemplate it, or decide to stiffen. It just happens. When we see something delicious, the body and mind tighten slightly to prepare to move toward it. We may not notice the tightening because our focus is on the situation out there and because the inner tightening can be subtle.

The tightening is not willful — it's not something we decide to do. It may be followed by thoughts and decisions. But tension itself is a preverbal, preconceptual, complex reflex. This tightening is the root of a sense of self — identifying various phenomena as part of "me" or belonging to "myself."

Taṇhā is often translated as "craving." It can be large and powerful, like a junkie with darting eyes and trembling hands craving her next fix. But it can also be as subtle as an inclination, as wispy as a soft yearning, as quiet as a niggling worry, as light as a fantasy. When we're bored, we may feel the mind thicken into a fog. These are different flavors of taṇhā.

## Abandon and Relax

How do we abandon tension? We relax. It's that simple. We relax the body, the emotions, the mind.

Notice that we don't abandon suffering; we don't try to turn away from it, rise above it, turn lemons into lemonade, push it under water, or grin and bear it. So it feels like relaxing into. We may relax into anger, relax into fear, soften into loneliness, let down into grief. Whatever comes along, we soften into it. We accept our experience without holding onto it or pushing it away.

Relaxing may not bring us immediate relief. But without tension, the suffering runs out of fuel. When there is no more tension, new suffering does not arise.

When we relax, we may even experience moments of pure awareness or awareness without an agenda or conditioning. The more we feel this ease, the more we suspect it's been here all along.

*It's as if we're in a classroom of rowdy kids who are banging chairs, throwing erasers, yelling, and punching. Over in the corner someone is writing poetry. We don't notice her because of the hubbub.*

*Then one morning we arrive early to class. The room is empty except for the young poet. We talk quietly with her or sit silently as she composes. Gradually the other kids enter with their boomboxes and carrying on. Soon the room is back to cacophony.*

*But now, even with all the noise, we can sense the poet because we know what our experience of her feels like.*

Like the poet in the classroom, pure agendaless awareness is always with us. Without the pure awareness, there'd be no awareness of any kind. Distorted awareness is pure awareness covered with junk.

What's pure awareness like without the junk? It's like asking, "What's the sky like without clouds?"

Let's experiment and see if we can get the clouds out of the way for a moment. Ready? Okay, now…

*STOP THINKING!…*

What happened? Maybe you were startled. Or felt irritated. Or amused.

But before you reacted, was there a flicker? A split second when the mind was blank for a moment? A tiny pause that went by quickly? What was that pause like?…

Maybe it was too short to tell.

Let's see if we can do the same thing in a gentler way.

*Sit with your lap exposed and your hand held up in front of your shoulder. Then let it drop freely to your lap.…*

*Now, do it again. This time, as your arm drops, drop your thoughts. Don't push them away or manage them. Just abandon them by letting them fall away the same way you let your arm fall.…*

*Do this a few times…*

Did you notice a moment when the mind was relatively free of content? The Tibetan Mahāmudrā tradition calls this the "natural mind."

After a short time, maybe less than half a breath, the thoughts start up again. But for a moment, the mind has no content, just pure awareness of awareness. This is peacefulness — awareness without tension or distortion.

*Now, relax as you look around the room. As you notice various objects, see if you can feel that quiet, open space of pure awareness — the natural mind — behind your thoughts and perceptions.*

*As you notice various thoughts and images in the mind, drop them and see if you can feel the awareness that holds them. It's like shifting your attention from the clouds to the sky. You don't even have to get rid of the clouds. Just notice the sky. Notice the space of the open mind…*

Pure awareness is not just an absence. It has a feel and texture of its own. It's peaceful, kind, vast, simple, wise, impersonal, and patient. It has many of the qualities associated with a benevolent God. You don't have to believe in God to feel them. Call it "God," "human essence," "Buddha nature," "mellowness," "the Force," "fairy dust," or "spadoodle." Those are labels and stories. The concepts aren't important. What's helpful is being with the experience itself: turning toward it and really letting your experience be whatever it is.

# Savoring

This brings us to the third practice: savoring peace, well-being, or other wholesome qualities. The text reads:

*Now this, monks, is the noble truth of the cessation of suffering: it is the remainderless fading away and cessation of that same craving, the giving up and relinquishing of it, freedom from it, nonreliance on it…*

*"This is the noble truth of the cessation of suffering": thus, monks, in regard to things unheard before, there arose in me vision, knowledge, wisdom, true knowledge, and light.*

*"This noble truth of the cessation of suffering is to be realized": thus, monks, in regard to things unheard before, there arose in me vision, knowledge, wisdom, true knowledge, and light.*

*"This noble truth of the cessation of suffering has been realized":
thus, monks, in regard to things unheard before, there arose in me
vision, knowledge, wisdom, true knowledge, and light.*

The phrase "remainderless fading away" means the taṇhā
ceases without a trace — nothing remains behind. In short the
Buddha is saying, (1) cessation happens, (2) realize when cessation
happens, and (3) cessation has been realized by me. If you do the
same thing, you'll get what I have gotten.

The text uses the word "realize" as in "make these qualities
more real by experiencing them directly." A simpler way to say this
is "savor the experience" — let it soak in.

There are various depths of realizing peacefulness. The first
comes from savoring quiet moments.

When we abandon tension, it subsides. The remaining
peacefulness may be so quiet that we don't notice it. The mind is
drawn to tension; peace has none. So awareness may slide right over
the peacefulness without noticing it.

Sitting in meditation or walking in the woodlands, sometimes
my mind becomes soft and luminous without my knowing it. I'm
more familiar with striving and figuring things out. Peacefulness
doesn't jump up and down and wave its arms crying, "Notice me!
Notice me!" Sometimes I'm oblivious to the glowing, lovely quiet.

It doesn't help to grab hold of the peacefulness. It does help to
enjoy it. This allows us to know it is real. As we savor the quiet, we
let the fleeting moments of stillness stretch out a little so we know
them better.

*When our kids were growing up, my wife Erika and I tried to keep them
away from soda and other sugar. But we didn't want them to develop a
complex about it. So once a week, they could have a small glass of soda.
Usually it was on Saturday morning.*

*Damon, our youngest son, would look at the little glass of cola, smell
it, feel the fizz on his cheeks, take a tiny sip, let it swirl around his tongue.
He'd close his eyes and savor it while it lasted.*

Savoring means absorbing the loveliness.

# Fading of Desire

As we savor peace and the kindness that grows out of it, it goes deeper, and we begin to realize where it came from. Imagine we've been hungering for something sweet all day. Finally we get a first bite of a mango or chocolate: "Ahh." The taste brings bliss — at least for a moment until we start hankering for a second bite.

The problem is that we may believe happiness comes from getting what we want. The advertising industry preaches the philosophy of getting what we want and getting rid of what we don't want.

But if we shift our attention from the chocolate or mango to the quality of awareness, we see that with the first bite, the hankering disappears. We no longer want it because we have it. Too often we confuse getting what we want with not wanting. So rather than savor that lovely state of mind, we focus on getting the next bite. Aversion and greed are back all too soon, and the bliss is gone.

A deeper contentment comes from realizing that the happiness didn't come from a mango tree or a cocoa bush. It didn't come from "out there." It came from "in here" when the mind-heart abandoned the tension of liking and disliking. Lao Tzu wrote, "We're rich when we know we have enough."

As desire fades and contentment grows, kindness makes more and more sense. This shift can feel dramatic, like Saul of Tarsus being struck by light from heaven on the road to Damascus. More often it is subtle, ordinary, and unpresumptuous, like seeing an old woman crying and being reminded of your grandmother: the only thing that makes sense is putting your hand on her shoulder and asking, "Can I help?"

Ralph Waldo Emerson wrote, "To know even one life has breathed easier because you have lived, this is to have succeeded."

With this we sense that the peace, well-being, and kindness has been with us patiently all along, like the poet in the classroom.

Can you feel it now?

# Contemplation

*Let your eyes close, or rest your gaze in some undistracted place…*

*Think of some difficulty in your life. Perhaps it's something that pulls your spirits down…*

*Let go of your stories and ideas about it. Let them wander off while you turn toward the feeling of the situation. What's its texture? What's it like inside? What's your mood as you look at it?*

*Do you notice any tension? It could be in your body, mind, or emotions…*

*If so, invite it to soften. Don't push the situation aside. Just let any tightness or thickness in your mind or heart soften…*

*If any relief or ease comes up or sits quietly in the background, relax into it. Savor it…*

*Smile a little. See how that feels…. Savor….*

# Inner Landscape

So far in this book, we've explored the value of befriending our inner experience. This includes appreciating the gift of vulnerability, the blessings hidden in so-called "hindrances," the different ways to engage and learn from our demons and difficulties, and the importance of kindness and a patient heart.

As we turn toward whatever life brings along, relax into it, and savor any peace and well-being that arises, we are not transforming ourselves into something new. We are patiently letting down into the heart and mind's nature.

As this befriending settles in, we are in a better position to explore the subtleties of our inner landscape. This landscape is the core of the Buddha's practice and the topic of this section.

# 5

# *Experience*

As we become friendlier toward our inner landscape, we notice more of its subtleties and nuances. At the same time, a deeper well-being begins to emerge. In this section of the book, I'd like to begin a multi-voiced conversation about our inner landscape. One of the voices is the Buddha's: he offered skillful guidance for investigating what we find inside.

However, the Buddha is no longer with us. All we have are his words. And those words were translated through various cultures and languages on their journey to the 21st century. Many experiences are too subtle to be easily put into words, even when we speak the same tongue.

So before exploring the inner landscape, it would be helpful to reflect on the nature of the language we use to convey experience.

## Water Goat

*My father was a marine engineer. During the middle segment of his career, he worked with a team of engineers designing oil tankers. He developed expertise on the giant steam turbines used to propel these ships. He worked for Esso International out of an office in New York City. However, he often traveled to Phoenix and Geneva, where the turbines were built. I was amused that the two places where engines for huge ocean-going vessels were assembled were about as far as one can get from the ocean: the Arizona desert and the Swiss Alps.*

*The technical papers, engineering specifications, schematics, and other documents coming out of Switzerland were in German. At that time, computers were beginning to be used for a growing variety of tasks. Someone wrote a program to translate these papers from German into English.*

*At first, the translations looked good. Some German syntax sounded awkward in English, but the documents were understandable. Except for one term. The translations kept referring to water goats. What was a water goat? No one knew.*

*They found an English-speaking engineer fluent in German and had him read the original papers. A "water goat" turned out to be a hydraulic ram.*

# Translations

Words have no inherent meaning of their own. They are fingers pointing to the moon, not the moon itself. Words are verbal or graphic symbols pointing to specific experiences. If you and I have a similar experience and agree to use the same word — let's say "gwauk" — to refer to it, then that word is helpful. "Gwauk" points to something with which we are both familiar.

But even within a single language, words typically have a cluster of meanings and connotations. The same word may be used to point to very different experiences.

The bark of a tree has nothing to do with the bark of a dog. The bark of a dog has only a superficial relationship to the way the drill sergeant gives orders. And none of these meanings have much to do with the peppermint bark I pick up in the candy store.

Still, if we understand the meanings surrounding a word, we can usually pick the correct one from the context.

When we try to translate from one language to another, the process is more complex. When my father told me about water goats, I understood for the first time that words do not have exact equivalents in other languages. The clusters of meanings and connotations are not the same in different languages. As far as I know, no single German word points to the skin of a tree, the yelp of a dog, abrupt orders, and a kind of candy.

We can't translate from German to English simply by finding the right English word for the German one as if there is an exact equivalent. We can't translate a Pāli term into an English word by looking it up in a table of word substitutions. What we do with a wet goat is very different from what we do with a hydraulic ram. To call the sergeant's orders "candy" is confusing at best.

Even if the translated word is kind of correct, subtle nuances can skew the meaning. For example, in English the phrase "come alive" is often metaphorical. The same phrase in Chinese is usually literal. When Pepsi started marketing in China, they used their very successful slogan "Come alive with the Pepsi generation." It translated into Chinese as "Pepsi brings your ancestors back from the dead." The slogan was not very successful in selling soda.

# Meditation

While learning to meditate, we may seek guidance from a man known as Siddhārtha Gautama, the Buddha — perhaps the most gifted meditation teacher the world has known. He lived and died 2,600 years ago in a different age, different culture, different economy, different worldview, different class structure, and different consciousness.[10] He spoke a language further from English than English is from German.

His talks were not recorded in the language he spoke. As best we know, he spoke a dialect of *Prakrit*. Centuries after his death, his talks were first written down in the *Pāli* language. *Pāli* and *Prakrit* don't have a word for *meditation*.

---

[10] In the Buddha's time, the most advanced stage of consciousness generally available was traditional literal consciousness — what we associate with fundamentalism. In the 21st century, the most advanced stages of consciousness are postmodern pluralism and integral consciousness. For a more detailed discussion, see Doug Kraft, "Stages of Consciousness," *Meditator's Field Guide*, pp. 263-268.

So when we turn to the Buddha for meditation guidance, we are looking for help in a process that he did not even have a word for!

The Pāli word usually used to translate the *Prakrit* word he used is *bhāvanā*. *Bhāvanā* was an agricultural term. It described what farmers do with their crops — caring for the soil and planting seeds. It might better be translated as "cultivation." It was a common, everyday word that implied helping something grow in a natural way. It connoted support, nurturance, and care.

The English word "meditate" has a slightly esoteric tone — something done by special spiritual people. But *bhāvanā* was an earthy term familiar to farmers and peasants. It is organic and grounded in everyday life. I'm not saying all this to discourage you — quite the opposite. It's amazing how much we can learn from the Buddha's guidance despite how far away he is in time, space, culture, worldview, and language.

But to get the most from what he says, it helps not to get caught up in nuances of English words. He did not speak English or Pāli. English nuances may be irrelevant.

It helps to remember that states of consciousness and qualities of awareness are far subtler than any words. It helps to remember the context of the Buddha's life, who he was speaking to, what their concerns might have been, and what his words might have meant to them. It helps to look at our own experience and intuit what he might have been hinting at. And it helps to let our thinking be a little loose as we feel our way through his words and our experiences.

# Three-Way Conversation

Keeping all this in mind, I'd like begin a conversation about the inner landscape we engage in during meditation — what we see when we turn our attention to our innermost mind-heart.

The Buddha will be one voice in this conversation: what he had to say about our experiences. We'll look at the Pāli terms and see if we can unpack what those words meant to the Buddha and to those around him.

I'd also like to bring science into this conversation. The Buddha encouraged us to look at our experience impersonally and objectively. Scientific language encourages us to think impersonally. We'll consider some of what we're learning from evolutionary psychology and the neurology of consciousness.

The result will be a three-way conversation between our innermost experience, the Buddha's commentary, and scientific observation.

# The Core of Buddhism

To start the conversation, let's consider what the Buddha thought was most important. He said, "I teach one thing and one thing only: suffering and the cessation of suffering."

Right away we have a problem. In English that sounds like two things. I think he was saying, "I'm only interested in alleviating suffering. But we have to understand what suffering is before we can know how to alleviate it."

The distinction is important. Buddhism can sound pessimistic because it looks squarely at suffering. But the Buddha never said "life is suffering," only that life has suffering. He was optimistic about our capacity to ameliorate suffering — which was his main interest.

# Suffering

Because he was most interested in mitigating suffering, our first question is, "What is suffering?"

We could respond: hurt, pain, hunger, wanting, desiring, fear, stubbed toes, broken hearts, grief, failure, and so on.

Notice that none of these say what suffering is. We all experience it, yet suffering is so hard to define that we often fall into describing its apparent causes and giving examples.

The Buddha did the same thing. In the text, he doesn't define suffering. Mostly he describes its causes and gives examples.

It's like trying to describe the color green. We might call it "yellowish blue." But that hardly conveys the experience. For me "yellowish blue" brings to mind a Cub Scout uniform with its blue shirt and yellow neckerchief: not helpful.

So instead we might say, "You already know what green is. You've experienced it. Green is the color of grass in the spring, leaves in the summer, bell peppers, the 'go' light on the traffic signal, clover." This is more effective than trying to define "greenness" abstractly.

In a similar fashion, when the Buddha described suffering he gave a string of examples: "Birth is suffering; aging is suffering; sickness is suffering; death is suffering; sorrow, lamentation, pain, grief, and despair are suffering; not to obtain what one wants is suffering; in short, the five aggregates affected by craving and clinging are suffering. This is called suffering."[11]

He's saying, "You already know what suffering is. It's what you experience with aging, death, sorrow," and so forth. He gives examples.

Suffering is intangible in the sense that it doesn't exist in physical, three-dimensional space. It's an inner phenomenon. It's something we subjectively experience inside. And we each experience it a little differently.

## Experience

This begs a larger question: "If suffering is a kind of experience, what is experience?"

*Experience* is harder to pin down than suffering. Yet Buddhism is all about experience — the intangible inner landscape. Another way to approach the question is to ask, "Who experiences?" For example, do our pets have experiences?

---

[11] "Sammā Diṭṭhi Sutta: The Discourse on Wise View," *Majjhima Nikāya* 9:15.

It seems like they do. They see, respond, remember, dislike things, want things. Even fish sleep — have stretches of not experiencing much — and later wake up and start having experiences. When I was a child dropping fish food into the fishbowl, they recognized what it was and swam toward it — they remembered and responded to stimuli.

## Flow of Information

Let's bring science into the conversation. First, a reminder of how our discussion has unfolded so far. We started with the Buddha's question "How do we alleviate suffering?" This led to the question "What is suffering?" It seems to be something we experience. This then led to the question "What is experience?" This is even harder to pin down. So we'll turn to objective science to see if it can help.

Neuroscientists have a working definition of experience that is worth contemplating: "Experience is the tip of the iceberg of the flow of information through us."

What does that mean?

Five hundred million years ago, jellyfish were the most complex creatures on the planet. They had specialized cells: some cells sensed light, some cells "tasted" chemicals in the water, some cells were muscles.

The information about what "tasted" good or bad had to be transmitted from the sensory cells to the motor cells that could move the jellyfish toward or away from food or threats. They developed other specialized cells for transmitting information from one part of the organism to another. That was the beginning of neural tissue.

Today, our bodies transmit a vast amount of information. For example, two million cells in our bodies die every second. Every cell in the body is replaced at least once every seven years. The body knows what to do about this. Various systems remove the dead cells and start new cells growing. This requires an ongoing exchange of information. Most of this communication is below the level of our experience.

What we actually notice consciously is a tiny fragment of all this information: sights, sounds, tastes, smells, touch, thoughts, moods, ideas, emotions, and more. Our nervous system does a lot to sort out and interpret information as well as pass it along.

Neural science says "experience" is the very top level of this transmission of information: signals that register consciously.

It's hard to know if a jellyfish actually has experiences or if it just responds mechanically to sensory information like a zombie. But more complex creatures seem to have experiences. They have all the underlying physiological mechanisms that support experience in us.

Crawfish and shrimp, to give one example, can be trained to move toward or away from various stimuli. To do this they must be able to sense things, remember them enough to associate them with other things, and act on that information.

Maybe they are zombielike, but it seems that they experience something. And their experience is based on this flow of signals through their systems. When I first heard Rick Hanson talk about these phenomena, it made sense to me. Rick is best known as the author of *Buddha's Brain*.[12] He is also a psychologist and dhamma student.

Examples of experience that we or other creatures might have include seeing, hearing, touching, smelling, tasting, thinking, yearning, reminiscing, worrying, planning, dreaming, and so on. Even our thoughts — whether we act on them or not — are the results of the processing of lots of information.

---

[12] *Buddha's Brain: The Practical Neuroscience of Happiness, Love and Wisdom,* New Harbinger Publications, 2009. A number of ideas in this section were stimulated by a talk of his I heard in April, 2017.

## Clusters of Experience (Khandhas)

Now let's bring the Buddha back into the conversation. He divided this flow of signals — that is, "experience" — into what he called *khandhas*. *Khandha* literally means aggregate, heap, cluster, or loose pile of similar kinds of experiences. A *khanda* is a cluster of a type of experience.

There are five kinds of *khandhas*. Everything we experience falls into one of them. We can use them to map our internal experience in meditation or anywhere in life. They underpin this thing called "suffering."

What's important is not the labels, but recognizing the states in our own inner experience. What are the phenomena these words point to?

Here are the five khandas the Buddha describes:

## Rūpa — Raw Sensation

The Pāli term for the first khandha is *rūpa*. *Rūpa* refers to a living, energetic, animate body with working sensory organs. *Kāya* is a Pāli term referring to the physical aspects of the body: bone, blood, tissue, and so on. A *kāya* can be a corpse. But *rūpa* refers to a live body with operating senses. A dead *rūpa* is an oxymoron. So while *rūpa* also could be translated as "body," it connotes the senses through which we know the body: seeing, hearing, touching, tasting, feeling, and thinking. *Rūpa* is raw sensation.

Optical illusions can help us distinguish *rūpa* from the other *khandhas*. Is the first image on this page a duck or a rabbit? Is the second Bill Clinton playing a saxophone or Monica Lewinski? Is the image on the next page an old cowboy or his son?

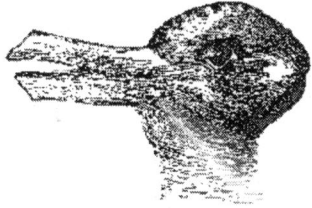

As you look at these images, what you think you see — duck or rabbit, saxophone player or woman, old man or young man — can change quickly from moment to moment. But the actual light patterns striking your retina do not change. The raw sensations caused by the light patterns are *rūpa*. Our interpretation is a different *khandha* that we'll get to shortly.

## Vedanā — Feeling Tone

The second *khandha* is *vedanā*. Even though it is often translated as "feeling tone" or just "feeling," it is not emotion. Emotions are complex, involving other *khandhas*. *Vedanā* is simple. It is one component of emotion, along with thoughts, beliefs, ideas, and more.

Classically, *vedanā* comes in three types. One is pleasant, one is painful, and the third is neither pleasant nor painful. However, there may be more than three kinds of *vedanā*.

As you view the three illusions, read these words, gaze out the window, or listen to the nightly news, you may experience different feeling tones.

The Buddhist texts do not include a lot about *vedanā*. But I've become convinced that it's crucial to a mature meditation practice and a rich life. I will go into this in more detail in the next chapter.

## Saññā – Perception or Labeling

The third *khandha* is *saññā*, or perception. In Buddhism, perception implies putting a label or a concept on an experience.

The meditation teacher and author Stephen Levine described taking some ornithologists on an excursion through a wildlife sanctuary. Stephen came to the job knowing little about birds. He wrote:

> *Walking with experts, they would say, "Ah, look at that vermilion flycatcher" or "Ah, there's a Canadian marsh hawk." And I started noticing, walking in the woods, that I would see "vermilion*

*flycatcher" instead of the crimson, living reality. "Marsh hawk"
instead of the truth.*[13]

His mind tightened as the labels covered and replaced the living experience and "pushed away the scintillating suchness of things."

Labels are real and can be directly experienced as thoughts, words, or images in the mind. But the labels themselves are not the content of raw experience. They are pointing fingers, not the moon itself.

Illusions demonstrate how *saññā* can change while the rūpa remains unchanged. The following scrambled letters also illustrate how what we physically see (*rūpa*) can remain the same while the *sañña* changes:

*Msot poelpe are albe to raed wrods as lnog ecah wrod has all the right letrtes and the frsit and lsat ltteres are in the rgiht pacels. Erevy tihng esle can be mexid up. I'ts aznimag how esialy the mnid oargneizs the rset itno fiaimalr pternats and maeinng. Tihs sohws the defrniecfe beweetn rpua khnada (raw senastoin) and sñaña khnada (prepcptnio). Rpua cahnges while sññaa sayts the smae.*

The *khandhas* interact with each other. I remember Joseph Goldstein telling a story that illustrates the complexity of these interactions. It went something like this:

*A couple moved into a new house. The first morning in the house, they woke to the sounds of birds chirping in their basement. They heard them on and off through the day and concluded the birds had a nest down there.*

*They were delighted. It felt like a blessing to have these woodland creatures take up residence with them. They decided to stay out of the basement lest they scare them off before the babies were grown.*

*However, a few days later, they had to go down to the basement to tend to something. The husband tiptoed down as unobtrusively as he could. He quietly looked around for the birds or their nest.*

*He saw nothing.*

---

[13] Stephen Levine, *Who Dies: An Investigation of Conscious Living and Conscious Dying*, New York City: Anchor Books, 1982, p. 31.

*Then he heard a loud chirp. He turned around. He was looking at a smoke detector. It chirped again.*

*The squawking of the defective smoke detector was so annoying that they called an electrician to come out as soon as possible and fix the darn thing.*

The actual sound they heard (*rūpa*) did not change. But their perception (*saññā*) as chirping or fire alarm did change. The feeling tone (*vedanā*) changed based not on the sound (*rūpa*) but on the perceptual interpretation (*saññā*) of the sound. This illustrates that the same raw sensation (*rūpa*) can have very different feeling tones (*vedanā*) depending on its label (*saññā*).

## Saṅkhāra — Stories and Concepts

The fourth khandha is *saṅkhāra*. It's a complex term with many different meanings. Loosely, it refers to thoughts, concepts, beliefs, stories, mental constructs, and ideas.

The term itself literally means something that has been pushed into form. *Khara* means "action," and *san* implies some extra push in those actions. It's about something being formed or molded.

In Pāli, the implication is that something that is formed is fragile. It can easily fall apart. The songwriter Paul Simon wrote, "Everything put together sooner or later falls apart."[14]

Because it's about something being formed, one common translation of saṅkhāra is "formation." However in English, "formation" sounds like a rock formation. It implies permanency.

Another increasingly popular term used to translate *saṅkhāra* is "fabrication." But that implies conscious intentionality, which may not always be true.

Evolution favors thinking (as described on pp. 46-47). For many millions of years, our ancestors were hunters and gatherers who mapped out the world around them to remember where food could

---

[14] This line appears in the song "Everything Put Together Falls Apart," which first appeared on his album *Paul Simon,* released in 1972.

be found and where dangers lurked. Primate children love to play and pretend — it's in our DNA. As they exercise their imagination they are developing skills that are helpful for exploring the environment.

So when there is any stress in the system, either positive or negative, the brain wants to mull it over or figure it out. We end up focused on what we're thinking about and miss the experience of thinking itself. We are drawn deeper into the storyline itself than into experiencing the nature of the thought. Nevertheless, thoughts do have preverbal feeling tones, textures, and moods that we can learn to see.

"The Room of Thought" is an exercise that illustrates thought as an experience in and of itself, separate from its content. It's easiest to do the exercise if a friend reads it to you slowly. But you can also read it through yourself and do it on your own. It goes like this:

*Close your eyes and relax for a few moments…*

*Imagine a room with two doors, one at either end. You are standing in this room near a wall so that you are about equal distance from each door.*

*Your thoughts come in one door, move through the room past you, and go out the other door. Take a few minutes to just watch the flow of thoughts as if they were visible in this room…. Notice what they look like…. Notice how they move…. They may come in different sizes, shapes, and colors…. Some may zip through quickly while others saunter along…. Some may float while others trudge….*

*Now the exit door closes. Thoughts can enter but can't leave. See how this affects them and what happens in the room….*

*Now the entrance door closes. Thoughts cannot exit and new thoughts can no longer enter. See what effect this has….*

*Now both doors open so thoughts can both enter and leave. Observe what happens now….*

*One thought slows down, stops right in front of you, and looks you over carefully. See what this is like….*

*Now imagine switching places so that you are no longer you observing a thought, but instead you are the thought observing you the person. What do you notice about your self?…*

*Imagine switching back to being you watching the thought. Has it changed through the experience?…*

*Now let the scene return to "normal" with you watching your thoughts move into and out of the room of awareness.*

In meditation it's important to notice the process of thinking, planning, conceiving, imagining, and so on apart from the content of the thoughts, plans, concepts, images, and the like.

Peaceful thriving requires unmasking thoughts to see them as they are and relaxing the tension they use to grab our attention.

## Viññāṇa – Awareness

The final khandha is *viññāṇa* or awareness. Viññāṇa has also been translated as "consciousness." In English, consciousness has two different meanings: (1) how we interpret awareness and (2) awareness itself.

How we interpret awareness is affected by contact (*phassa*) between a sensory stimulus (like light), a sensory organ (like the eye), and a sensory awareness (like seeing). It can also be affected by all the other *khandhas*. So consciousness is conditioned by sensations, feeling tones, perception, and stories. It includes all the other *khandhas* within it.

Therefore, I think translating *viññāṇa* as awareness gives a better understanding of this *khandha*. I think of it as "knowingness," "awareness," or "pure awareness" that has no agenda.

Here is an exercise that illustrates and sorts out these various meanings.

*Take a few moments to settle into a quiet space.…*

*Now place your awareness on your foot. See what you notice.…*

*Now place your awareness on the places where your body touches the chair.…*

*Now bring your awareness to the sensations of the breath.…*

*Notice the sounds from the street.…*

*Notice the temperature of the room.…*

*The colors on the walls....*

Were you aware of your foot in the few moments before I mentioned it? Probably not. The foot was there. It followed you into the room. But subjectively it was not there until you put your attention on it.

This illustrates that awareness has two aspects. One is the object — the foot, the body where it touches the chair, the sounds, and so on. And the other is awareness itself. Without awareness, you would know nothing of your foot, the sounds from the street, the pictures on the wall.

However, evolution bred us to attend to the objects and to ignore the awareness. To survive in a difficult situation, it's more important to know the environment than the awareness itself. That is why it is easier to focus on an object, like the sensations of the breath, rather than on awareness itself.

To thrive rather than merely survive, we need to be aware of the awareness. Meditation is not about the object. It's not about the breath, a mantra, a feeling of mettā, a kōan. It is about awareness itself. It's about seeing the qualities of the mind-heart and how they shift and change.

How do we do this? To illustrate, let's continue with the exercise:

*With your eyes open, let yourself settle in again for a few moments....*

*Now be aware of sight — know that you are seeing. Rather than get entangled in what you see, just be aware of seeing....*

*Now be aware of sound — that hearing is happening. Let go of the interpretation of the sound and be aware that you can hear and are hearing....*

*Now be aware of awareness in a more general way. Perhaps you are aware of sights or sounds or temperature or sensations inside the body, or many things at once. But also know that you are knowing. Be aware of awareness....*

*It's miraculous. We can be aware! Notice if you can notice being aware....*

Were you aware of seeing itself — not the object but the actual seeing — before I asked you? Probably not.

How much energy did you expend becoming aware of awareness? Pretty close to zero.

It does take effort to remember to be aware of awareness. But it doesn't take much energy. That is the secret. Wise effort is very light and relaxed. It can be deliberate but has no tension.

## Summary

We haven't answered the question "How do we relieve suffering?" We haven't even answered the question "What is suffering?" other than to say it's a kind of experience. But we have begun to answer the question "What is experience?" When we look at our inner landscape, everything we experience falls into one of the five *khandhas*.

I skipped lightly over the second *khandha, vedanā*. It's important, and it's been overlooked. So we'll spend the next chapter on *vedanā*. After doing that, we'll have a better map of our inner experience and can ask, "What turns experience into suffering?"

But before leaving the *khandhas* in general, I want to suggest that the *khandhas* themselves are important if for no other reason than to say, "Don't confuse one kind of experience with another."

For example, if you ask me what I'm feeling and I say I'm feeling like people don't understand me, I have not actually told you what I feel. I've stated an interpretation of what other people might be doing (not understanding me), not how I feel about it (mad, sad, glad, scared, confused…). I've substituted a thought (*saṅkhāra*) for a feeling tone (*vedanā*). Thoughts are easy to see. *Vedanā* is subtle.

Yogis often confuse one *khandha* for another, in particular confusing thoughts and ideas with other kinds of experience.

The Buddha said that if we can just know what's going on inside, that's enough to awaken us. If we know what's going on, the mind knows what to do about it. But we have to know it on its own terms. We have to know it as it is in and of itself, not as we think it is or interpret it to be.

In the "Satipaṭṭhāna Sutta" (*Majjhima Nikāya* 10), the Buddha says we must know feeling as feeling, perception as perception, thought as thought, and delusion as delusion rather than substitute our thoughts for our feelings or labels for sensations. In verse 34 he asks, "How does a person abide contemplating mind as mind?" Because we experience the mind as a field of awareness, the Buddha is asking, "How do we abide knowing awareness as awareness?" He answers his question:

> He knows mind affected by lust as mind affected by lust, and mind unaffected by lust as mind unaffected by lust. He knows mind affected by hate as mind affected by hate, and mind unaffected by hate as mind unaffected by hate. He knows mind affected by delusion as mind affected by delusion, and mind unaffected by delusion as mind unaffected by delusion. He knows contracted mind as contracted mind, and distracted mind as distracted mind. He knows exalted mind as exalted mind, and unexalted mind as unexalted mind. He knows surpassed mind as surpassed mind, and unsurpassed mind as unsurpassed mind....

He advises knowing things on their own terms. This includes knowing awareness as awareness.

Awareness is a fundamental property of the universe. By "fundamental" I mean it cannot be split into subparts. We can break down an automobile or a flower into lots of constituent parts, but we can't break awareness down into anything else. It is fundamental.

And one of the mysterious properties of clear awareness is that it soothes, quiets, and opens the mind-heart. We don't have to do it. All we have to do is see things as they are — know delusion as delusion, hate as hate, kindness as kindness, and awareness as awareness.

Awareness of awareness is subtle, so along the way we may work with various objects to help the mind settle enough to see awareness. But in the end, awareness of awareness rather than just awareness of the object is what's most important.

Awareness of awareness can't be forced. But it helps to recognize it as it emerges. We swim in a sea of awareness. Kabir said, "I laugh when I hear the fish in the sea are thirsty."

If you can't directly know the knowing right now, don't worry. As awareness gets stronger, it will emerge all by itself. We swim in it all the time.

# 6

# *Feeling Tone*

*Note: About half of this chapter appears in* Meditator's Field Guide *(pp. 67–71) and is repeated here for continuity.*

In the last chapter, I began exploring the inner landscape — what we find when we look inside. I organized this exploration as a three-way conversation between our experience, the Buddha's commentary on experience, and the sciences of neurology and evolutionary psychology.

I began with the question, "What is suffering?" At the very least it is something we experience. This begs the question, "What is experience?"

The Buddha suggested that experience could be categorized in five different *khandhas* or clusters. I went through all five. However, I said little about the second khandha, *vedanā*, or feeling tones.

This chapter picks up the conversation and looks at vedanā in detail. It's important to remember that even though vedanā is often translated as "feeling tone" or just "feeling," it is not emotion. Emotions are complex. Vedanā is embedded in emotions. But vedanā itself is just pleasant, painful, or something else that is neither.

## Pluto

Vedanā reminds me of Pluto: it is faint and difficult to see. Pluto was first discovered not by

viewing it in a telescope but by inference. Slight variations in Neptune's orbit could only be explained by the presence of an unknown celestial body of sufficient mass to distort Neptune's path. Similarly, we may first notice vedanā by how it draws our attention to various phenomena.

When I was growing up Pluto was the ninth and outermost planet in our solar system. However, it's not very big: one-sixth the mass of our moon. So, in 2006 it was downgraded to a dwarf planet — too small to be a real planet but too large to be an asteroid.

In an analogous way, the charge in vedanā is not big enough to be *taṇhā* (craving) and not small enough to be just raw sensation. It falls between the two.

Raw sensation, vedanā, and taṇhā are part of dependent origination: a more detailed and dynamic version of the khandas that we'll explore in Chapter 9, "Holding Dear" (pp. 135–156). For now it's enough to note our organism is bombarded with lots of sensory information every minute. Most of it flies below the radar of conscious awareness and passes by unnoticed. Vedanā is a signal that says "pay attention to this." The signal is not yet strong enough to say "do something." It just says "notice."

For example, I was meditating one morning when I heard a squeak and a clunk. My mind went gently to the sounds and put together a story: my wife was in the kitchen feeding our cat. The squeak was from a hinge on the cupboard door where the cat food is stored. The clunk was from a spoon hitting the porcelain cat dish as she served the food.

That little draw of attention to the squeak and the clunk was vedanā. There was more charge in it than sound alone. But not enough to motivate me to do anything except pay attention long enough to know there was nothing I had to do. Once I understood, the vedanā relaxed and my attention came back to my meditation practice. Meanwhile it was raining outside. There must have been sounds of water in the roof gutters. But there was no vedanā with those sounds— they didn't draw my attention.

# Stepchild

Vedanā is the stepchild of the khandhas. It has been misunderstood and overlooked. However, I'm coming to believe it is central to developing an effective meditation practice and a happy life.

When the Buddha said "All things converge on vedanā" (*Anguttara Nikāya* 9.14), he was suggesting that vedanā is pivotal in our experience. It's one of the five khandhas. It's the seventh link of dependent origination — right in the middle where it gives rise to *taṇhā* (craving). It's the second of the Four Foundations of mindfulness. The four are body sensation, feeling tone (vedanā), mind, and mind objects. This means vedanā is a primary object for mindfulness training.

Despite its importance, the text includes little about it. For example, the "Satipaṭṭhāna Sutta" (*Majjhima Nikāya* 10) goes on for many pages about the first, third, and fourth foundations. But the second foundation, vedanā, has only two verses, 32 and 33. In their entirety they read:

*32. And how does a person abide contemplating vedanā as vedanā? [That is, knows feeling tone directly on its own terms rather than through some other frame of reference.] Here, when feeling a* **pleasant vedanā***, they understand: 'I feel a pleasant vedanā'; when feeling a* **painful vedanā***, they understand: 'I feel a painful vedanā'; when feeling a* **neither-pleasant-nor-painful vedanā***, they understand: 'I feel a neither-pleasant-nor-painful vedanā.'*

*When feeling a* **worldly pleasant vedanā** *[pleasant sense experience without taṇhā], they understand: 'I feel a worldly pleasant vedanā'; when feeling an* **unworldly pleasant vedanā** *[non-sensory or upper jhāna experience without taṇhā], they understand: 'I feel an unworldly pleasant vedanā'; when feeling a* **worldly painful vedanā***, they understand: 'I feel a worldly painful vedanā.' When feeling an* **unworldly painful vedanā** *[hindrance when in a jhāna], they understand: 'I feel an unworldly painful vedanā'; when feeling a* **worldly neither-pleasant-nor-painful vedanā** *[confusion or indifference], they understand: 'I feel a worldly neither-pleasant-nor-painful vedanā'; when feeling an* **unworldly neither-pleasant-nor-**

*painful vedanā [equanimity], they understand: 'I feel an unworldly neither-pleasant-nor-painful vedanā.'*

33. *"In this way they abide contemplating vedanā as vedanā **internally**, or they abide contemplating vedanā as vedanā **externally**, or they abide contemplating vedanā as vedanā **both internally and externally**. Or else they abide contemplating in vedanā **their nature of arising**, or they abide contemplating in vedanā **their nature of vanishing**, or they abide contemplating in vedanā **their nature of both arising and vanishing**. Or else mindfulness that 'there is vedanā' is simply established in them to the extent necessary for bare knowledge and mindfulness. And they **abide independent, not clinging to anything** in the world. That is how a person abides contemplating vedanā as vedanā.*

That's it. The text doesn't even have my bracketed asides or highlights. The "Vedanā Samyutta" (*Samyutta Nikāya* 25.5) has a little more text, but it doesn't offer more explanation. We don't find much about vedanā elsewhere.

The terms "pleasant," "painful," and "neither-pleasant-nor-painful" might suggest they are on a spectrum from pleasant to unpleasant. So I used to mush them all together into a scale that runs from pleasant to neutral to unpleasant, or from delight to neutral to yuck.

But the Buddha's language suggests that there are actually three different kinds of vedanā experience: pleasant vedanā, painful vedanā, and a third vedanā that is neither of those.

Remarkably, 2,600 years after the Buddha, neural science supports what the Buddha said: there are entirely different systems in the body for each of these three. So, let's look at what science has to say about them.

In the last chapter, we noted that neuroscience suggests experience arises out of the information flowing through our system. More information flows through our system than we can possibly attend to. Vedanā may be a signal that says, "This information is important. Pay more attention."

## Painful Vedanā

Painful vedanā signals threat — a safety concern or imbalance that may need attention. This might be a threat to physical integrity: there's a bear in the front yard or there's a rattlesnake on the path. It might be a momentary psychological imbalance resulting from an insult or something being out of place: "Who put the glass in the wrong cupboard?" "Daddy, Billy is putting his hand on my side of the car seat!"

A neural system in the body specializes in picking up signals of pain and threat. We experience these signals as fear, aversion, anger, hatred, uneasiness, imbalance, and so forth.

All these are painful even if they aren't physically painful (yet). They may only be mentally uncomfortable. They alert us to a possible danger and push us toward fight or flight.

These signals are sent (mostly) to the most primitive part of the brain — the lower brainstem. Indeed, painful vedanā feels primal.

## Pleasant Vedanā

Pleasant vedanā relates to something the organism needs or wants in order to feel satisfied: food, sleep, water, shelter, sex, and so forth.

Another neural system in the body specializes in picking up signals of pleasure. When this system is activated, pleasant vedanā lures the organism toward an object to satisfy the need.

These signals are sent (mostly) to the brain's limbic system. When satisfied, the brain tends to release dopamine.

We experience these signals as liking, sweetness, desire, pleasure, and so forth. They create a kind of stickiness of mind that stays with a pleasant object.

## Neither-Pleasant-nor-Painful Vedanā

Neither-pleasant-nor-painful vedanā arises when the body is awake but the mind is not. The need for safety, satisfaction, or anything else is dormant. The pain and pleasure systems are quiet.

There is very little signal of any kind. The brain's arousal systems are quiescent.

When the mind is quiet, attentive, relaxed, undisturbed by pain or pleasure, it can become quite equanimous. We feel comfortable.

However, because we aren't paying attention, we risk missing something important or falling into delusion or confusion. We may miss a threat to our safety or an opportunity to satisfy a need. Without any arousal, we can be quiet, relaxed, and inattentive without awareness. This is unwholesome vedanā that is neither pleasant nor painful.

We may experience this vedanā as boredom, stupor, thickness or density of mind, inattentiveness, lack of presence, ho-hum mind, fogginess, indifference, confusion, fatigue, dreaminess, and more.

### Connection Vedanā

There may be another kind of vedanā that Rick Hanson calls a need for connection. It is not neutral. It has an arousal quality that can be positive or negative. So it sounds like painful or pleasant vedanā. However, it doesn't deconstruct into a need for safety, satisfaction, or mental attentiveness.

In evolutionary terms, it seems to be more recent — emerging in higher mammals in the last million years or so.

For example, I heard about a guy on a whale watch who saw three grey whales protecting seals from being eaten by several orcas. He wondered what would motivate whales to take care of seals? What's the evolutionary advantage of that?

One advantage is complex but compelling. Intelligent species have complex brains that take a long time to mature. Because they rely more on intelligence than hardwired instincts to survive, they are relatively helpless until they learn and mature. Bees are born adults. But humans, great apes, and whales (to name a few species) have prolonged childhoods. They depend on parents for protection and wisdom in order to survive. Without their parents' care and compassion, intelligent children would not grow into adults and pass along their DNA.

One primary attribute of intelligence is flexibility — the capacity to adapt and learn from experience. So in intelligent creatures, caring and compassion are not narrowly focused. They are generalized and may arise in many situations.

Protecting seals provides no specific evolutionary advantage for whales. But there is a huge advantage for a generalized instinct to care for smaller, more helpless creatures.

So, wired into us is a huge sensitivity to children and especially babies. If we show a human a picture of a baby person, monkey, lion, wolf pup, horse, bird, or turtle, we think they're cute. From a human perspective, there is nothing cute about a baby turtle. But recognizing it as a young animal can trigger feelings of warmth, caring, and protection.

All intelligent species seem to have a deep sensitivity to relationships, even to creatures who are a different species. I woke up one morning to find Lila, our feline family member, curled up next to me, her body pressed against my chest, her front paws on my shoulder, and her chin resting on my chin. She was fast asleep.

This fourth vedanā is more complex than the first three and probably relates more to the higher brain centers. The neocortex comes much later in evolution. Connection vedanā may not be possible without a neocortex of some significance. It can be a strong urge or weak, positive, or negative. Depending on life experience, it may be strengthened or weakened. But it seems necessary for survival of intelligent creatures.

As noted earlier, connection vedanā doesn't really deconstruct into a need for safety or a need for satisfaction. It's experienced as an urge to connect — to be in heartfelt relationship with another person or group of people. Without enough connection, connection vedanā may be experienced as loneliness, isolation, or disconnection. One of the most painful experiences for a human may be being shunned, ostracized, or rejected. But it's not the same pain as hitting your thumb with a hammer. If we have a falling out with a close friend, we may describe our inner state as threatening. But it's not the same kind of threat we feel from a wolf running toward us. If we have a lovely evening with a close friend, we may call it "pleasant" or "satisfying." But it's not the same pleasant sensation we chocolate lovers get from a piece of chocolate.

After hearing Rick Hanson talk about the possibility of connection vedanā and exploring it in my own practice, I spoken with several other teachers about it. None of them accepted it. They see it as a variation of the three classical types of vedanā.

However, I do notice in my meditation that many of my random thoughts are in the form of explaining something to somebody. Sometimes there is an earnestness in my inner voice wanting to connect with the person I'm talking with in my mind. It's as if I want the person to understand me so we'll connect a little more.

Perhaps I'm hypersensitive to relationships. Or maybe there is some of this in all of us. Whether we think of it as a fourth vedanā or just a variant of the first three, I have found it very helpful to be more attentive to how it works.

## Buddha

References to vedanā and connection vedanā may not be found in the text very often. But they aren't completely absent either. Here is a passage from the "Maggasamyutta," *Saṃyutta Nikāya* No 41.2(2):

> *Thus have I heard. On one occasion the Blessed One was dwelling among the Sakyans where there was a town of the Sakyans named Nāgaraka. Then the Venerable Ānanda approached the Blessed One. Having approached, he paid homage to the Blessed One, sat down to one side, and said to him: "Venerable sir, this is half of the holy life, that is, good friendship, good companionship, good comradeship." "Not so, Ānanda! Not so, Ānanda! This is the entire holy life, Ānanda, that is, good friendship, good companionship, good comradeship. When a bhikkhu has a good friend, a good companion, a good comrade, it is to be expected that he will develop.*

The Buddha seemed to place a lot of importance on healthy, heartfelt compassion. Still, the Buddha was a guy. We know there are statistically significant differences between how the brains of men and women generally function.  So he may not have emphasized relationship as much as he would have if he had been a woman.

Or maybe relationships aren't emphasized in the text because his teachings were passed down through patriarchal cultures that stressed individuality more than relationship — the Buddha's teachings about relationship may have been diminished by unconscious bias.

Considering these possibilities, it may be helpful to reflect on connection vedanā and whether there is a distortion in the transmission of the Buddha's teachings that could be corrected.

## Vedanā Meter

Remember that vedanā signals a need for safety (from a threat or imbalance), satisfaction (of a need), clarity (in an ambiguous situation), or connection (with others). We tend not to notice the signal because we're too busy acting on it.

If a saber-toothed tiger walks up the path and we get engrossed in how awful that makes us feel inside, we're more likely to be eaten than if all our attention is riveted on the tiger. If we see a lovely piece of fruit and get engrossed in how delicious it might taste, some other creature may get it before us. If we see a beautiful/handsome person and get engrossed in how good that makes us feel, they're more likely to pass us by than if we attend to them.

So these signals impel us to quickly focus attention on the beast, food, or person rather than our inner feelings. We may not notice the vedanā.

The Buddha suggested it is very helpful to see vedanā as vedanā — to notice the signal itself apart from the object that triggers it. But he didn't offer any specific techniques for doing it. We may have to come up with our own.

Here's a simple technique created by one of my teachers, Tony Bernhard. He calls it a "mental app," which he's named "The Vedanā Meter." Rather than installing the app on our smartphone, we install it in our mind. His version focuses only on the pleasant and painful dimensions of vedanā. Here's how it works:

We walk into the doctor's office and say "My foot is sore." The doctor asks, "On a scale from 0 to 10 where 0 is pain-free and 10 is excruciating, how intense is the pain?"

After a moment's reflection, it's easy to give numbers: "In the morning, it's usually a 2. In the evening it's a 6. Right now it's 4.5." Those numbers are measures of painful vedanā.

We could also set up a measure of pleasantness. On a scale from 0 to 10 where zero is boring and 10 is total delight, how is eating a cookie? Petting a kitten? Spring flowers? Your favorite music?

The Vedanā Meter has both scales. The pain scale runs from pain-free to the worst intensity we could experience. The pleasant scale runs from ho-hum to the loveliest rush we could know.

For the sake of simplicity, we might combine both scales into one that runs from intense pain on one end to neutral in the middle and intense pleasure on the other end.

To create your Vedanā Meter, imagine such a scale in your mind. You can design it any way you like. Tony's looks like a circular car speedometer. Zero on the left is the most painful. Ten on the right is the most wonderful. Five in the middle is neutral.

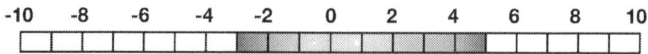

When I first tried this exercise, the image that popped into my mind was a horizontal bar that ran from -10 on the left (torture) to 0 in the middle (neutral) to +10 on the right (total delight). Another yogi's Vedanā Meter resembled a stereo equalizer with different scales for different frequencies.

The mental images are just metaphors. So use whatever comes most naturally for you. Once you have mentally created your meter, the next step is to "calibrate" it. Here's one way to do it:

*Close your eyes for a moment and bring an image of your meter to mind. Then have a friend read the following words to you. Or if you're alone, you can read them to yourself.*

*Notice how your meter responds to each of the following. What's important is not what you think about the phenomenon but how pleasant or painful it feels. See how these register on your meter:*

*Chocolate ice cream*
*Child on a swing set*
*A glass of milk*
*A hug*
*In-laws*
*Jimmy Carter*
*Your father*
*Public speaking*
*Dog poop*
*Donald Trump*
*Sun on your face*
*Your first-grade teacher*
*Stubbing your toe*

Once you're familiar with how your meter responds to a variety of experiences, you're ready to bring it into meditation and into your life. For example, what does your meter register right now? Then notice it in other situations as you move through your day or as various objects come to mind in meditation.

When I first tried out my app, it seemed pretty simple — perhaps even simplistic. But the results were unexpected. To my surprise, I found I'm basically happy most of the time. My meter is usually in the 3 or 4 range. As the day flows along, it sometimes dips to a -4 or -5. Sometimes it rises to a 6 or 7. But mostly it hovers in a moderately positive range.

This realization threw me a little. If you ask me at a random time how I'm doing, the first thoughts that pop into my mind are complaints. Those negative thoughts are the product of childhood conditioning a long time ago. Yet today, my thoughts still tend to say "I'm a -2 today" when my actual Vedanā Meter is usually more of a +3. I didn't realize how different my thought content could be from my mood.

Another surprise was how much I enjoy thinking. While meditating, I often view a thought sprint as an annoyance. But when I'm thinking, the meter can go up to a 6 or 7. The thought content can be negative, while the process of thinking can be pleasurable.

Seeing how pleasurable thinking can be has made it easier to not fight thoughts. I understand the mind's attraction to them. Rather than push them away, I can take in the pleasant vedanā and release the thought content. The underlying uplifting quality can be healing if I don't fight it. I don't have to get lost in the content of the thoughts. That content can be released. I just rest in the pleasantness behind the specific thoughts and let it radiate outward.

Another observation I've made and heard from others concerns what happens when vedanā is in the negative range. If I see the feeling tone with dispassionate interest, the meter tends to move in a positive direction on its own. For example, if I'm feeling sad and openly recognize the sad feeling itself without getting into a story about it, it tends to lighten up a little.

I've come to appreciate that vedanā — the preverbal painful and pleasant dimensions of everyday experience — may be so subtle as to go unnoticed. Yet it may reveal tantalizing insights if we learn to listen to its moods with an opening heart and a quieting mind.

## Tanhā Meter

As mentioned earlier, one difficulty in recognizing vedanā is that it is a signal that can trigger an urge. The Pāli terms for these urges are *taṇhā* (unwholesome desire) or *chanda* (wholesome desire).

Psychologists and neural scientists call these "drive states" — we want to do something and are gently or strongly urged to act. If the drive is for safety or balance, the vedanā signal will be unpleasant: pain, fear, aversion, or anger that urges us to fight or flee. Anger tends to trigger aggression. Aversion tends to trigger flight.

If the urge is for satisfying a need, the vedanā signal will be pleasant: a sweet desire or wanting that draws us toward the object. If the urge is for connection, the vedanā signal might be loneliness or disconnection.

In short, the signal (vedanā) that can trigger a drive state (*taṇhā* or *chanda*) moves us toward or away from the object. The drive state itself (chanda and taṇhā) can be so strong that it masks the vedanā. We are less conscious of the signal, and more conscious of the object or the drive to move toward or away from it.

Nevertheless, it is possible for something to be strongly negative and slide off us like water off a duck. And it's possible for something to be strongly pleasant without driving us to act.

So, it's important to be able to notice not only how painful or pleasant something is but also how strong the urge is to do something about it. Some things can be very pleasant, but I'm fine whether I have them or not. Sometimes I'm compulsively driven. And sometimes I'm in between.

*Taṇhā* is a good candidate for a mental app. Tony Bernhard calls it a "Wanting Meter." Rather than measuring pain or pleasantness, it measures the intensity of desire or aversion — wanting something or wanting to be rid of something.

We can create a Wanting Meter, or Taṇhā Meter, in a manner similar to how we created a Vedanā Meter: First, produce a mental image of a scale that runs from powerful aversion to neutral to powerful desire. Then add numbers to the scale. That's it.

The Wanting Meter may not need to be pre-calibrated. We pre-calibrated the Vedanā Meter by thinking of various painful and pleasant sensations and seeing how the meter responded to each. But the intensity of wanting is not tied as directly to raw sensations. For me, chocolate often produces pleasant vedanā. Sometimes I crave chocolate; other times I can take it or leave it. The pleasantness of chocolate may stay the same, but the strength of the desire can vary widely. An insulting remark might trigger hatred or mild annoyance or indifference, or even slight pleasantness that someone is actually paying attention to me. Thoughts might be fueled by a powerful craving to solve a problem or by a faint wondering.

Because the intensity of desire or aversion for a specific object can vary, pre-calibrating the Taṇhā Meter may not be necessary. We can simply start using it.

# Vedanā Meter 2.0

The Vedanā Meter I described does not envision all aspects of vedanā — just the painful and pleasant dimensions. Adding a few other aspects to the Vedanā Meter gives rise to version 2.0.

### Relational Vedanā

As I became aware of the possibility of relational vedanā, a little checkbox appeared next to the meter in my mind. If the vedanā had anything to do with relationships — even if only the mind explaining something to someone — that little box was checked. Sometimes, instead of a checkbox, there was a light that was on or off.

### Neither Pleasant nor Painful

It took me a long time to realize that neither pleasant nor painful vedanā was not just a zero point on the pleasant or the painful scales. It's a catch-all category for anything that can gently draw our attention away without being pleasant or painful. Neither pleasant nor painful can refer to mild curiosity, confusion, dullness of mind, indifference, or other states that are not compelling but nevertheless influence attention. This could be called neither pleasant nor painful vedanā.

At that time, my mind often became thick and foggy. So I added another scale that went from clear mind to dense mind.

But adding that to the mental image made it more complex. The complexity became a distraction. So I dropped it but remained attentive to how clear or blurry awareness was even without a new scale.

Depending on your temperament, you may find it helpful to upgrade your Vedanā Meter to version 2.0 that includes a relationship relevance indicator or other scales. Or you may find it more helpful to keep it simple.

## Freedom

Without the urge to move away from or toward an experience, there would have been no evolutionary advantage to the vedanā signal. So once an urge is active, the signal has done its job and may recede into the background. That is one reason vedanā is hard to notice.

Taṇhā is the weak point in the chain of dependent origination.[15] The Buddha emphasized that this is very important. It's the easiest place to release tension and stop the flow toward suffering.

When we relax tension, we may notice the vedanā — the signal that triggers the taṇhā. With that awareness, we become familiar with a place before the taṇhā arises. Vedanā contains a tiny bit of tension. If we can see it and relax, taṇhā is stopped before it even starts.

We don't have to alleviate suffering. All we need to do is Six-R it. That relaxes the tension before suffering arises. With that, we are on the path to true freedom.

---

[15] See chapter 8, "Hidden in Plain Sight" and chapter 9, "Holding Dear" for an in-depth discussion of dependent origination, pp. 111–148. For now, think of it as a string of causal relationships.

# 7

# Dissolving Suffering

This is the third chapter in this section on the inner landscape. The section opened with the Buddha's central questions, "How can we relieve suffering?"

To answer this, we have to know "What is suffering?" Since suffering is something we experience, this begs a more basic query, "What is experience?"

To answer this, the last two chapters explored the Buddha's five *khandhas*, or clusters, of experience: *rūpa* (body sensations), *vedanā* (feeling tones), s*aññā* (perception or labeling), s*aṅkhāra* (thoughts, beliefs, mental constructs, stories), and *viññāṇa* (awareness itself, without which we'd know none of the other four *khandhas*). Taken together, these five khandas include everything we can experience.

Now we can reframe the question "What is suffering?" as "What turns experience into suffering?"

## The Buddha

To respond to this, let's see what the Buddha had to say. Earlier I quoted the "Sammā Diṭṭhi Sutta: The Discourse on Wise View" (*Majjhima Nikāya* 9:15), where he said:

> Birth is suffering; aging is suffering; sickness is suffering; death is suffering; sorrow, lamentation, pain, grief, and despair are suffering; not to obtain what one wants is suffering;

We noted that these are not a definition but examples of suffering. The Buddha then offered a definition:

*In short, the five aggregates (or five khandhas) affected by clinging are suffering. This is called suffering.*

I skipped lightly over this definition because we needed to understand the five khandhas first. Now that we've done that, let's unpack his definition: "khandhas affected by clinging."

"Clinging" is a translation of the Pāli word *upādāna*. Clinging/*upādāna* is the way the mind shrink-wraps around an experience and gives it a label. We experience *upādāna* as a thought. It's the beginning of words and concepts.

Because the khandhas include everything we can experience, the Buddha is saying anything we experience that is affected by clinging is suffering. Anything the mind grabs hold of or pushes away creates suffering. In other words: *clinging turns experience into suffering.*

Where does clinging/*upādāna* come from?

In the Buddha's Map of dependent origination, clinging is always preceded by *taṇhā* (craving) — a preverbal, instinctual tightening. The second Ennobling Truth says our experience of suffering is rooted in *taṇhā*. Clinging creates suffering. And clinging has roots that go down into *taṇhā*.

Where does *taṇhā* come from?

In dependent origination,[16] taṇhā is always preceded by vedanā – feeling tone that is pleasant, painful, or neither pleasant nor painful. Dependent origination gives us this sequence: vedanā can trigger *taṇhā* (craving), which can trigger clinging (*upādāna*), which we experience as suffering.

What is vedanā?

---

[16] In chapter 8, "Hidden in Plain Sight" and chapter 9, "Holding Dear" I'll discuss dependent origination, pp. 111–148. For now it's enough to note that it's a string of causal relationships. In this case, taṇhā is caused by vedanā.

Vedanā is a kind of experience. As noted earlier (p. 72), neuroscientists define "experience" as the tip of the iceberg of the information that flows through the body systems. More specifically, vedanā is a signal that something needs attention.

Vedanā itself has no particular charge. It's just a message, like "Houston, we have a problem." On the Apollo 13 mission to the moon, the astronaut Jack Swigert felt an explosion and observed warning lights. We wouldn't have blamed him for yelling, "Yikes, we're all gonna die!" But his training to see objectively and impersonally kicked in. He calmly signaled there was a concern that needed attention: "Houston, we have a problem."

Vedanā is like that. It's calm information without tension. If the information is about a threat ("There's a rat in the closet"), the signal is an uncomfortable mental experience: fear, anger, imbalance. If it's a need-satisfaction concern ("I haven't eaten in a while"), the signal is a pleasant feeling toward an object such as food. If it's a connection concern ("I've been alone for a while"), the signal is a thought or feeling about people.

Vedanā can quickly trigger taṇhā, which can bring a very large charge to our experience. But the vedanā itself is just flat, emotionless information.

To summarize, vedanā (feeling tone) can lead to taṇhā (craving or tension), which can lead to upādāna (clinging). The Buddha said suffering is any experience affected by clinging. Notice that it is possible to experience vedanā without suffering. But once upādāna arises, we suffer. Taṇhā floats in a grey area in between which is not suffering but can easily lead to suffering. We'll come back to this important point shortly.

# Baked In?

But first, here are some other interesting questions: "Can we survive without suffering?" "Is suffering essential to life as we know it?" "Are bummers baked into life as we understand it?"

The Buddha gave two answers: "Yes" and "No." "Yes: *dukkha* (suffering) is embedded in the relative world in which we live. It's unavoidable." And "No: we can attenuate and dissolve suffering."

## Serenity

To untangle this seeming contradiction, consider an allegory from the 2005 science fiction movie *Serenity*[17]:

*Hundreds of years in the future, humans are terraforming planets to support human life. On the distant planet of Miranda, a colony introduces Pax G23 into the air filtration system. Pax is a new drug designed to suppress aggression and make people happy.*

*Communication from the colony stops. The authorities assume there has been an invasion or natural disaster, or that the Pax23 has backfired. The "23" in the name suggests there were earlier versions that didn't work.*

*Through a series of adventures, the movie's lead characters arrive on Miranda. They find everyone dead. There are no signs of invasion, natural disaster, poisoning, or violence. A woman apparently died while leaning against a library window. A man lies smiling and dead on the floor of a public building. Others died sitting in chairs or lying in the grass. Corpses are everywhere.*

*Eventually they figure out that Pax had worked too well. It had removed aggression and any emotion that might lead to aggression: hatred, anger, desire, greed, wanting, yearning, caring, hunger. The people became so peaceful and unmotivated that they stopped working, socializing, eating, or even moving — they just sat down and died.*

In normal, everyday life, the complete absence of desire would be a complete disaster. Like the people on Miranda under Pax G23, we'd not be motivated to turn off the stove, feed the children, come out of the rain, get out of bed in the morning, or even eat. We'd waste away and die. Just consider what you've done today. If you were not motivated to do anything, what would your day have been like? Would it be worth living?

---

[17] This movie summary and a more detailed exploration of wholesome and unwholesome desires appears in Doug Kraft, "Unhealthy Desire vs. Health Wisdom," *Meditator's Field Guide*, p. 79–82.

Yet the Buddha discovered that the roots of suffering are taṇhā and its three flavors: want, aversion, and delusion. These roots can give rise to clinging, which is where suffering begins.

We can make a good case for the necessity — perhaps even the goodness — of suffering. Without some discomfort, we might not live long enough to experience much of anything. As the meditation master Sayadaw U Tejaniya puts it, "Suffering gives us motivation."

Yet, the Buddha also says it's good to end suffering.

## Signal vs. Charge

Allowing for the difficulties of translating from the Buddha's spoken Prakrit to written Pāli and from Pāli to English, I think he was saying there's a difference between a signal of pleasure, pain, or neither pain nor pleasure on the one hand, and the drive, urgency, or motivation to do something about it on the other hand. We can't live without vedanā. We can't live without the signals in our system that alert us to a possible threat or opportunity. We also need enough motivation (*chanda*) to do something about it. But if we're skillful and wise, the signal and motivation don't have to tip over into clinging and suffering.

## Our Experience

Let's consider this in our own experience. As noted earlier, we can eat ice cream, find it pleasurable, crave more and suffer. We can also eat ice cream, find it satisfying, and feel no need for more. We can experience pleasure without suffering.

We can sit in the meditation hall as someone tiptoes past and think, "They're disturbing my meditation. I wish they'd stop stomping around!" We feel aversion which can trigger clinging and suffering.

We can also sit in the meditation hall as someone enters and lets the door slam. If our equanimity is strong, we hear the sound pass through us but remain undisturbed. We don't suffer.

Yogis who have meditated for years often report that they've become sensitive to subtler signals. Colors are brighter, nuances of feeling are clearer, flavors are more pronounced. And at the same time, over the years they have found themselves feeling more and more comfortable in highly charged situations.

My therapist turned to me once and said, "Doug, it's only pain." I thought, "Oh yeah. Right. It *is only* pain. What's the big deal?" She helped me see that I could observe huge charges without being thrown off balance.

Those who work with the Vedanā and Taṇha Meters (pp. 85–99) find that signals of pain and pleasantness are different from the urgency to do something about them. They aren't the same thing. Without urgency, there is more equanimity and less suffering.

I trained and worked for years as a bioenergetics therapist. Bioenergetics is a form of psychotherapy that pays close attention to the way energy runs through the body. From my work on myself in psychotherapy, as a psychotherapist, in meditation, and as a meditation teacher, I've come to an understanding of suffering that is in harmony with both modern psychology and ancient Buddhism:

When the strength of a signal and the charge around it is within the range of what we can manage gracefully, we don't suffer.

When the charge is more than we can gracefully manage, our system gets overwhelmed. Chanda (wholesome instincts) becomes taṇhā (craving, aversion, confusion), which triggers upādāna (clinging) and we suffer.

# Alleviating Suffering

With this understanding of suffering, I'll return to our starting question: "How do we dissolve suffering?"

I'll bring science back into the conversation by restating what I just said in the language of neurology.

Throughout the day, sensory information as well as thoughts, feelings, plans, ideas, beliefs, and so on are being passed through our bodies via the nervous system, blood chemistry, and probably other subtler systems. Mixed in with this information are drive states, signals for energy to be released, instructions to move various muscles, and so forth.

Most of this information is below conscious awareness. Some is not. If the drive states are too weak, we become docile, like the people on the planet Miranda. If the drive states are too strong — more than we know what to do with — our system is overwhelmed and suffering arises.

# The Middle Way

The question becomes how do we create the conditions in which we have enough drive to move around and live fulfilling lives but not so much tension that we suffer? How do we find this middle way?

Here are a few examples of what can be involved in finding that middle way in real life:

*I grew up in Houston, Texas within biking distance of the Sheraton Hilton hotel. It had a large, Olympic-size swimming pool including a ten-meter diving platform. On many summer days, my friend Bruce and I rode over there to swim.*

*Jumping off the ten-meter platform was scary. Our velocity when we hit the water was considerable. Doing a belly flop was extremely painful — it could knock the wind out of us, or worse.*

*Yet we leapt off the platform all the time. At first, we jumped feet first to be safe and get a feel for it. Later we just dove headfirst. As we did, anxiety arose in the background. To not have any worry would have been crazy.*

*Yet we had a great time. Jumping off that high platform was not suffering. We learned how to manage safety needs enough to stay within the range of what we could handle and still enjoy the lovely thrill of it all.*

Here's another example:

*Over the years of growing up, I built 20 or 30 tree houses. Only we called them "tree forts" – "houses" were for girls, "forts" were for boys in those days.*

*My friend Lindsey had a 75-foot oak tree in his yard. We built a fort 25 feet off the ground. A narrow limb rose off one side of the fort. I built a crow's nest toward the top of that limb. There was nothing but empty space between that little platform and the ground 50 feet below.*

*Sitting in the crow's nest, I was getting signals about danger and safety – my heart often pounded. But I learned to manage those signals well enough to have the time of my life.*

Here's another example: imagine driving down the interstate at 65 miles per hour in four tons of steel as other cars whiz past. If somebody wanders a few feet over the white line, we'll go up in a fireball.

Yet we can mostly manage traffic without suffering. If we had no concern at all, we'd be insane. But we can usually manage it well enough to remain alert without going over the top into stress and suffering.

# Equanimity

So the question of alleviating suffering is not how to get rid of vedanā — it's just a signal. It's not even how to get rid of taṇhā — that is just tension that can keep us on our toes when appropriate. It's how to manage the situation without tipping over into suffering.

This is an operational definition of equanimity — how we meet the challenges of life without numbing out or stressing out. The Buddha called this "The Middle Way." How do we have full, rich experiences without going into suffering?

Wilhelm Reich once said, "Anxiety is excitement without oxygen." If we relax into high-energy states and breathe easily, they are just energy and excitement. If we tighten up, they turn into anxious clinging and bummers.

The Buddha offered an image of how to dissolve suffering: if we stir a teaspoon of salt into a glass of water, the water becomes so salty we can't drink it. If we stir that salt into a large body of water, we don't notice it.[18]

The Buddha suggested that life has its teaspoons of salt. Life has its stressors. For some it is only a half-teaspoon. For others it may be a few tablespoons. However, the larger our container, the less the stressors affect us.

Making the container bigger is the solution. Making the container bigger is the key to equanimity.

Equanimity doesn't come from fortifying ourselves against life. It comes from expanding to include more and more. There are three ways to go about feeling better:

1. Reduce the amount of salt. This doesn't work so well. We have only a little influence on the world around us. But ultimately the world doesn't care what we want it to be. It is what it is.

2. Numb out our sensitivity to salt. In other words, we can dull ourselves with drugs or distractions, or by purposely focusing attention elsewhere.[19] This doesn't work so well either. We can numb out and push unpleasantness aside a little bit. But ultimately we don't really have that much control over our bodies. They obey universal, impersonal laws.

3. Make our container bigger. As Suzuki Roshi put it, "The best way to control a cow is to put it in a larger pasture." Making our container bigger is not always easy. But when meditation works, that is what happens.

## Three Essential Practices

To expand our container, the Buddha recommended three essential practices. There are lots of ways to implement them. But without all three, we are ripe for suffering. The third practice is

---

[18] "Lonaphala Sutta: The Lump of Salt," *Anguttara Nikāya* 3.99.
[19] Some meditation practices do this by focusing exclusively on a single object like the breath or a mantra.

especially important. All three[20] are introduced in chapter 4 (pp. 52–59) and discussed at length in *Meditator's Field Guide*.[21] For now I'll remind you of the first two and then look at the third in more detail.

### Turning Toward

The first essential practice for expanding our container is turning toward whatever life brings our way. The Buddha articulates this in the first Ennobling Truth. He said we must understand suffering. We can't understand suffering if we're busy fighting, running away, controlling, or fixing it. We have to turn toward suffering and learn how it arises, hangs around, and fades away. We must get to know instinctively how it works.

### Relaxing Into

The second essential practice in the Buddha's meditation is relaxing into whatever tension we experience. The second Ennobling Truth is that our experience of suffering is rooted in taṇhā — the preverbal, pre-conceptual tension that gives rise to clinging. The practice the Buddha assigned to taṇhā is "abandon." We are to understand suffering (the first ennobling truth). But we are to abandon taṇhā (the second truth). If we abandon the taṇhā, it doesn't progress into clinging and suffering.

To abandon taṇhā, we relax. It helps to say "relax into" to be clear that relaxing is not a means of relaxing *away* from suffering or *avoiding* bummers. It's a way to be with them and to be relaxed and open at the same time. Over time this allows our container to expand.

## Savoring

The third essential practice is savoring. If we turn toward and relax into, we may experience peace, well-being, uplift, or other

---

20 They are described in the Buddha's first successful teaching and recorded in the "Dhammacakkappavattana Sutta," *Samyutta Nikāya* 56.11. They are also discussed online at https://www.dougkraft.com/?p=TurningToward.
21 Doug Kraft, "Three Essential Practices" in *Meditator's Field Guide*.

wholesome, healing qualities. In the text of the third Ennobling Truth, the Buddha says we are to "realize" these uplifting qualities while they are present – to savor them while they last and let them seep into our bones. In this way we realize that they are real.

All states are temporary. They come and go depending on conditions. We have gotten pretty good at finding uplifted states. Using meditation, therapy, groups, music, yoga, exercise, art, drugs, entertainment, and so on, we can find ways to touch good feeling states. But we aren't so good at savoring.

How do we go beyond temporary relief from suffering to a deeper, more continuous abiding in well-being? Rick Hanson and others refer to this as "turning states into traits."

Savoring helps by allowing us to embody the experience. It doesn't help to try to grab hold of good experiences or try to hang onto them. It also doesn't help to pass over them without letting them sink in a bit. The Buddha offered a middle way: savoring the uplift while it's here. Knowing that it is real, or realizing it by enjoying it and letting it soak into the mind and body.

One of the Buddhist term for this is *nāmarūpa*. *Nāma* means "mind." *Rūpa* means "body." There is no "and" between the two words. *Nāmarūpa* is "mind-body" as a unified system. Savoring involves the mind-body.

Insight Mediation (*Vipassanā*) is pretty good on the mind side of *nāmarūpa*: insight, recognizing, seeing things as impersonal, and so on. But it's not so good at allowing these insubstantial mental qualities to seep down into the underlying body — helping the fleeting states become embodied underlying traits. The Buddha said the way to do this is to savor the *brahmavihāras* or other uplifted qualities when they arise.

It turns out that there are more uplifted qualities than contracted ones in the text. Here are a few of the uplifted ones:

### The Brahmavihāras:
*Mettā: Friendliness*
*Karuṇā: Compassion*
*Muditā: Joy, especially in response to someone else's good fortune*
*Upekkhā: Equanimity*

## Spiritual Faculties

*Saddhā: Faith, confidence, trust*
*Viriya: Energy without strain or push*
*Sati: Awareness, mindfulness, heartfulness*
*Samādhi: Stability of mind, collectedness*
*Paññā: Wisdom*

## Awakening Factors

*Dhamma vicaya: Curiosity, investigation of mental phenomena*
*Sati: Awareness, mindfulness*
*Viriya: Relaxed and open energy without strain or push (as above)*
*Pīti: Joy*
*Passaddhi: Calm, tranquility*
*Samādhi: Stability of mind, collectedness*
*Upekkhā: Equanimity*

## Others

*Gratitude*
*Forgiveness*
*Contentment*
*Love*

For most of us, incorporating any of these qualities into our practice makes meditation easier. One way to do this is to cultivate awareness alone. As awareness deepens, it will pull in other uplifting qualities. However, most people find it easier to intentionally incorporate other uplifted qualities from the beginning of their practice. The Buddha often seemed to have favored this approach.

Another reason savoring uplifted qualities is so important is that the brain is as much as four times more sensitive to negatives than positives.[22] This ingrained tendency to hang onto the negatives helped our ancestors adapt when we were a marginal species in a world of giant predators. It helped us survive.

But today, when we are at the top of the food chain, fixating on negative thoughts doesn't help us thrive. Expansive states pass through us quickly while negatives leave a more durable impression.

---

[22] The negativity bias has been studied extensively. A good summary found at https://www.en.wikipedia.org/wiki/Negativity_bias provides an overview and lots of footnotes.

By intentionally savoring expansive qualities, we build inner resources and become more resilient. When a difficulty comes along, we have more space inside — more equanimity — to greet the signals for safety, satisfaction, or connection without freaking out, running away, or going numb. We can get hungry and be okay with being hungry until we can get some food. We can manage our safety needs without getting hysterical or uptight. We can manage rough spots in relationships without flying off the handle or sulking away in silence. We can manage relationship conflicts without being conflict avoidant.

## Cultivating Grace

Another way to describe savoring is "cultivating grace." Think of grace as anything we are able to enjoy that we don't have to earn. This includes simple things such as air, sunlight, natural food, good company, a clear sky on a starry night, and so forth. We don't have to have any particular theology or belief system to realize that life offers a lot that we can enjoy without first earning it.

The *Brahmavihāras*, spiritual faculties, and awakening factors are examples of grace that are present all the time though we may not always feel them. They may be beneath the tension that draws our attention away from them.

Because these qualities are already quietly in the background, we can't create them. But we can make ourselves more sensitive to noticing them by quieting down, opening up, and listening. This makes our system more responsive to the pleasantness around us and more resilient when caught in the unpleasant.

## The Six Rs

Another way to savor wholesome qualities, cultivate grace, and deepen equanimity that I mentioned (pp. 17–19) is to use the Six Rs. Consider:

**Recognize** is about turning toward what arises.

**Release** is about letting go of storylines and letting go of controlling, managing, fixing, or tweaking our experience. This allows us to recognize it on its own terms.

**Relax** is about letting down into our experience, whatever it is, so we can release the tension without turning away from it.

**Re-Smiling** or bringing in uplifted qualities is part of savoring.

**Return** brings us back to our home base of radiating uplifted qualities. Returning deepens equanimity and encourages us to expand out of our seemingly small containers.

**Repeat** builds patience and equanimity.

# Cultivating Equanimity

Nothing in wholesome practice is about intentionally trying to stop desires or needs. The practice is about seeing desires and needs effectively — how they arise, hang around, and fade — and knowing how to relate to them wisely. The practice is not about getting rid of them. It's about wisely relaxing the tension or drive in them.

As equanimity gets stronger without becoming one-pointed on a single object, awareness opens and becomes more sensitive. We notice subtler and subtler signals and tensions that used to fly below the radar. The tensions may become easier to see and relax into even as they affect us less and less.

As meditation practice goes very deep, sensory information — as well as other signals and tensions — begins to fade away completely. This fading away can be fascinating and can bring us into a whole new world that has always been under our noses, too close to see.

Eventually tension and other signals fade completely. This helps cultivate the deepest kind of equanimity and the deepest kind of resilience: dispassion. In Buddhism, dispassion is interest in what happens without preference for any specific outcome.

This kind of dispassion dissolves suffering.

# 8

# Hidden in Plain Sight

Now we come to the heart of the matter. We've been exploring the inner landscape with particular attention to the experience of suffering and how it can be attenuated. In this chapter and the next, we'll turn to the core of the Buddha's teaching on this and everything else. It's called "dependent origination" or "dependent co-arising" (*paṭiccasamuppāda*). The Buddha said, "One who sees dependent origination sees the dhamma [or the whole of his teaching]; one who sees the dhamma sees dependent origination."[23]

The Buddha intended dependent origination to be a practical tool for cultivating awareness rather than a theoretical construct. To introduce it as a tool, let me first introduce you to the research of Eugene Gendlin, a non-Buddhist philosopher and psychotherapist.

By the 1960s, there were three branches of psychotherapy in the United States. Within each branch were many distinct schools. The oldest branch was psychoanalysis. It included Freudians, Jungians, neo-Freudians, Reichians, and more. A second and newer branch

*Paṭiccasamuppāda* is a Pāli term that has been translated as "dependent origination," "dependent arising," "interdependent co-arising," and "conditional arising." All these are valid and useful even though some seem to contradict others. (See "10. The Paradox of Paticcasamuppāda," pp. 157-160 for a more detailed exploration.)

---

[23] "The Greater Discourse on the Simile of the Elephant's Footprint: Mahā-hatthipadopama Sutta," *Majjhima Nikāya* 28:28.

was Behaviorism, including John Watson's classical conditioning, B. F. Skinner's operant conditioning, William Glasser's reality therapy, and others. The newest branch was the emerging so called "third wave" of humanist psychology, which included Abraham Maslow's hierarchy of needs, Carl Rogers' client-centered therapy, Fritz Perl's gestalt therapy, and Rollo May's existential therapy, to name a few.

Eugene Gendlin looked at this proliferation and asked, "Which therapy gets better results?" After years of careful research, he found that theoretical orientation made little difference. In all the schools, some clients did well, while others did not do so well.

So he honed in on the common elements in the experience of those who flourished. He found that if there was something in the therapist-client interaction that helped clients feel their own experience more deeply and intimately, they did well. If not, they didn't do so well. Gendlin called these nonverbal, bodily intuitions "felt sense." In 1978 he published a small, best-selling book called *Focusing*[24] that describes how to discover and cultivate felt sense.

In the mid 1980s, I met a colleague who had trained with Gendlin. He taught me focusing techniques. I found them remarkably effective with meditators as well as with therapy clients. At that time, mindfulness had not broken into the field of psychotherapy. But it was clear to me that awareness and insight were keys to both. The focusing technique bridged and connected the two.

I was so enthusiastic about Gendlin's process that another colleague and I began to expand the technique. As it evolved we called it "deepening."

# Buddhism

Today Buddhism is in an analogous situation. There are three main branches: Theravada, Mahayana, and Tibetan. Within these

---

[24] Bantam New Age Books, 1982.

branches are many schools. In all branches and schools, there are meditators who do well and meditators who don't do so well.

I suspect that if there is something about how meditators engage their practice that helps them sense their own experience more deeply and intimately, they do well. If not, their practice goes flat. For example if a meditator has preconceived ideas about what she should experience and looks for validation, she won't go very far. Nobody exactly fits any mold. However, if meditators are curious and are open to being surprised or perplexed, they are more likely to go further regardless of the flavor of Buddhism they use. After all, the Buddha's dying instructions were "Be a lamp unto yourself." He encouraged us to trust our own deepest experience first and foremost.

When the Buddha said seeing dependent origination is the backbone of his teaching and practice, the word *seeing* did not mean "intellectual appreciation." When we really see someone, we see more than a diagnostic category. We see them from the inside. We know how they tick, what inspires them, what frightens them, what they love, what wakes them in the night, what touches their heart. When the Buddha said, "See dependent origination," he meant an intimate, deep, direct contact with the subtleties of how life flows through us.

More than any other Buddhist teaching, dependent origination lends itself to getting lost in concepts and disconnected from direct experience. The key to effective use of dependent origination is not memorizing a list of Pāli names or their meanings. At different times, the Buddha described dependent origination as having four, eight, twelve, or more stages. However, all his descriptions move from gross to subtle, selfing (preoccupation with a personal self) to selflessness, tension to ease, and suffering to gentle freedom from distress. This overall direction is what's most important.

As with Gendlin's discovery, if we use dependent origination to help us directly touch subtle, precognitive experiences, then awareness deepens, insights emerge, and our engagement with life opens and enriches. If our use of dependent origination does not bring us into direct contact with intuitive knowing, it is little more than a flow chart on a blackboard. It may be impressive but has little practical effect on our meditation or daily lives.

## Causal Relationships

The essence of dependent origination is that everything depends on something else to cause it to arise (see "The Paradox of Paticcasamuppāda," pp. 157–160). Or more simply, everything arises from causes and conditions. Those causes and conditions arise out of other causes and conditions. And so on.

Dependent origination is a string of causal relationships. Picture a line of dominos. One falls, knocking over the next one, which knocks over the next, and so on down the line. In dependent origination, the first domino is so tiny we may not notice it. Each successive domino is a little larger. The last one is the whole catastrophe: pain, anguish, grief, despair, and bummers of all varieties.

Nature has many such causal chains that interact in a matrix in which everything directly or indirectly affects everything else. The Buddha said that understanding intimately the nature of these causal relationships is the key to his teaching, the key to meditation, and the key to spiritual freedom.

*Hetupaccayo* is a Pāli term for "causes and conditions." *Hetu* means "primary cause" and *paccayo* means a "supporting condition" that contributes to produce an effect or "fruit" (*phala*). Though it is often translated as "causes and conditions" there is no "and" in the Pāli term. It is a compound word combining the meanings of both to indicate all causes or conditions essential for a given result. A traditional example is a seed that is the main cause of a tree and the soil, sunlight, and water that are supporting conditions that allow the seed to germinate and grow. All causes and conditions must come together for the tree to come to fruition. *Hetupaccayo* is more precisely translated as "causesconditions." But this sounds clumsy in English.

## Trigger versus Causes and Conditions

To use dependent origination as a practical tool, it helps to distinguish between the root or necessary causes and conditions of an event, and the unnecessary triggers that merely set it off. The distinction between causes and conditions is somewhat arbitrary. Causes arise and pass relatively quickly. They are easy to see. Conditions change relatively slowly. They tend to linger in the background where they are easy to overlook.

Triggers, on the other hand, may merely carry a root cause. Triggers themselves are not strictly necessary. Here are two examples:

(1) I throw a match into a field of dry grass. A wildfire ensues. If someone asks, "Why is the field on fire?" our first thought might be the match. But if the match is removed, the fire continues.

The real and necessary cause of the fire is heat. The match carried heat, but once delivered, the match itself became superfluous. The root conditions are fuel and oxygen. If heat, fuel, and oxygen are present — if they co-arise together — we have a fire. If we remove any one, the fire goes out. The match was merely a trigger that brought heat to dry grass. Once the fire is going, it provides its own heat and will keep blazing until the fuel is burned up, removed, or turned into wet grass.

If the fire was a candle, we could also put it out by removing the heat (for example, blowing on it to cool it off) or removing the oxygen (for example, covering it with a jar). But for the brushfire, the only practical solution is to deal with the grass.

Once it's pointed out that necessary conditions include not only heat but fuel and oxygen as well, we think, "Oh yes. Of course." That's typical of conditions. Initially they can be easy to miss. But once we see them, they're obvious.

Fire is a good metaphor for suffering: once triggered, it can keep burning until we recognize and deal with the true causes and conditions. This brings us to the second example.

(2) Someone says, "Doug, your talk was dumb." While meditating early the next morning, my mind grumbles, "Was my talk dumb? Am I stupid? Maybe that person is dumb. Maybe I should tell them to 'be nice!'" Rumble, rumble, rumble. I'm overrun with hindrances.

If you ask me why I'm upset, I'll probably point to the person and their insulting remark. But the person and their editorial aren't in the room as I meditate. They are long gone.

The comment was only a trigger. It implanted an irritating thought in my mind. The real cause was the mind's ability to fixate on something painful. Once there, like the heat in the field, it carried on by itself. The necessary conditions are my ego defensiveness and underlying irritability. It's easy to overlook the role of my disposition. But once I see it, it's obvious.

To reduce the suffering in our lives, it makes some sense to remove the triggers: put away the matches, avoid crass people, turn off the nightly news, and avoid things that might upset us.

However, the world has an endless supply of matches, cigarette lighters, lightning strikes, downed power lines, and hot sparks of all kinds. It has an endless supply of insults, slights, thoughtless remarks, political inanity, and commentary on political inanity. And no matter how carefully we eat, exercise, and rest, we get sick, age, and die.

If we want peace and well-being that is more than a fleeting moment, it is wise to attend to the underlying conditions within us that make us vulnerable to the slings and arrows of the world. The Buddha encouraged us to look beyond mere triggers to what makes suffering possible and likely. To be skillful in the use of dependent origination, he suggested that the most important aspect is not what triggers suffering, but the conditions that allow suffering to continue.

Ānanda asked the Buddha, "Venerable sir, in what way can a monk be called skilled in dependent origination?" Notice the question was not "What is dependent origination?" It wasn't a philosophical inquiry. His question was "How can one use it effectively [as a practical tool]?" The Buddha replied, "Here, Ānanda, a monk knows thus: 'When this exists, that comes to be; with the arising of this, that arises. When this does not exist, that does not come to be; with the cessation of this, that ceases.'"[25]

In the statement, "this" means "causes and conditions." If we replace the word "this" with the phrase "causes and conditions," the phrase must be slightly modified to make sense. We end up with four statements: (1) if **all** causes **and** conditions exist, the result exists, (2) if **all** causes **and** conditions arise, the result arises, (3) if **any** cause **or** condition does not exist, the result does not exist, and (4) if **any** cause **or** condition ceases, the result ceases.

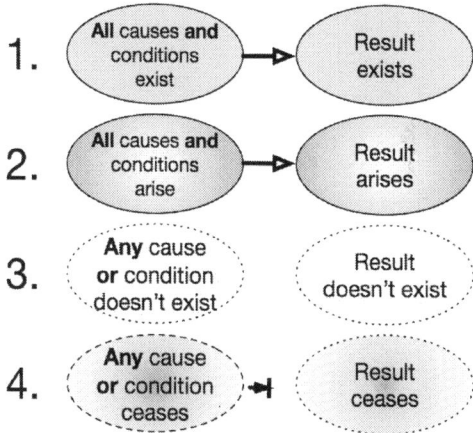

The most important statement is the fourth. Throughout the suttas, the Buddha advocates using dependent origination from the perspective of cessation (action 4 in the diagram on the preceding page). Because the Buddha was interested in relieving and eradicating suffering, he asked, "What cause or condition, if removed, results in the cessation of suffering?"

In the brush fire example, if all three causes and conditions (heat, fuel, and oxygen) co-exist together (action 1), the fire exists. If all three co-arise together (action 2), the fire arises. If any one of them does not exist (situation 3), there's no fire. Removing the match won't stop the fire! It was only a trigger. However, if any one of the causes or conditions (heat, fuel, or oxygen) ceases (situation 4), the fire goes out and will not restart.

---

[25] "Bahudhātuka Sutta: The Many Kinds of Elements" (*Majjhima Nikāya* 115:11).

## Vexing

Remember, dependent origination is a causal chain, not a single interaction. So to attenuate the conditions leading to suffering, we might ask, "What causes and conditions motivated me to throw the hot match into the grass?" Perhaps I was angry, upset, delusional, or wanting to get some attention. We could also ask, "What are the conditions that made it possible for me to throw a match?" These include owning a bike, liking to ride it, living near a dry field, owning matches, the invention of matches, knowing how to use matches, and more. We could also ask, "What are the causes and conditions that created the dry field?" They include the nature of grass, seasonal drought, global warming drying the field, human dependence on fossil fuels that exacerbates warming, seasonal shifts in weather, and more.

The Buddha said that trying to understand the chain of all the causes and conditions that give rise to a specific event is vexing — a polite way of saying it will drive us nuts. In the interdependent web, the combination of forces that give rise to a particular incident are potentially so numerous, varied, and complex that we don't have enough information or brainpower to figure it all out. He called such subjects "imponderables" (*acinteyya*) — topics that are not wise to pursue.

It sounds like he's saying his core teachings on dependent origination are imponderable and not worth pursuing!

# Hidden in Plain Sight

To tease apart this apparent paradox, it helps to engage dependent origination less as a theory and more as a practical tool

> *Acinteyya* is translated by different scholars as "imponderable," "inconceivable," or "unconjecturable." In describing the last two of the four *acinteyya*, the Buddha said, "The result of karma is an imponderable matter that one should not try to ponder... Speculation about the world is an imponderable matter that one should not try to ponder. One who tries to ponder [these] would reap either madness or frustration." "Acinteyya Sutta: The Four Impoderables," *Anguttara Nikāya* 4.77.

for awareness that can help us directly experience relevant subtle causes and conditions that may be hiding in plain sight. A story illustrates how they can be both obscure and apparent at the same time:

*When my boys were young, the Easter Bunny used to take the eggs the boys had decorated and hide them in the yard. On Easter morning, the boys took their Easter baskets outside and scoured the yard for colored eggs. They looked under bushes, inside watering cans, and behind rocks. They found none!*

*The Easter Bunny always hid the eggs in plain sight. A yellow egg might be placed among yellow flowers. A red egg might be sitting in a red toy truck. A green egg might be laid on top of a tuft of new grass. All the eggs were in plain sight, but placed so that they blended in with the yard and drew no attention.*

*When the boys figured this out, they would stop, relax, and gaze openly around the yard. Then they saw eggs everywhere.* [26]

Some of the root causes and conditions can be so subtle that we don't notice them. We need a sensitive and patient awareness that can relax and see those faint causes and conditions right under our noses.

# Tools and Techniques

Here are three tools that work together to help reveal what may be hiding in plain sight. The tools are felt sense, pointers, and deepening. Some come out of Gendlin's work. Others come out of my explorations. All of them have been shaped implicitly or explicitly by the Buddha's teachings on dependent origination.

### Felt Sense

The first tool is Gendlin's "felt sense." Here's an example:

Erika and I have been married for almost five decades. When we got married, I couldn't imagine what it would be like to be 48 years old much less to live with someone for 48 years.

---

[26] This story can also be found in Doug Kraft, *Buddha's Map*, p. 75.

After all these years I have a pretty good felt sense of who she is: big heart, grounded wisdom, smart, kind, attuned to the communities around her, strong presence, moved by music, and more.

How I feel about her might shift from day to day: affectionate, irritated, comfortable, concerned, close, wanting more space, and so on. My feelings *toward* her may fluctuate, but my felt sense of *who she is* remains relatively steady.

Whether we're considering a person, a situation, or a hindrance, our felt sense is subtler and less colorful than emotions. But it's more important because it sets the framework for how we see that person, situation, or hindrance. "Felt sense" is another word for "conditions."

In meditation, if we have a recurring hindrance, it may be because we are attending too much to the more obvious surface attributes and less to the underlying felt sense of the whole experience.

To get a feel for the difference between emotion and felt sense, try this:

*Choose a person, situation in life, hindrance, or just how this moment feels. Close your eyes and notice how you respond or react to the person, situation, hindrance, or moment. Notice if this response seems stronger in some part of your body or if it's dispersed....*

*Now notice your subtler, quieter felt sense of the person, situation, hindrance, or moment.*

Because emotions fluctuate more often, they are easier to see than felt sense. But if we sit quietly, we can begin to notice the difference between our emotional response to a person or experience and our underlying felt sense of that person or experience.

## Pointers

In the previous exercise, you may have noticed the power of language — the words we use to denote an experience. Once we put a label on something, the label can take over and detach from the underlying felt sense. Gendlin refers to the labels as "handles." I prefer the term "pointers," as in "It takes a finger to point to the moon, but don't confuse the finger for the moon."

Gendlin's way of working with handles is to go back and forth between the word (handle or pointer) and the direct experience.

For example, a yogi asks, "Fear has come into my meditation. What do I do with it?"

I might ask, "Does it seem to reside more in one part of the body?"

Then I suggest, "'Fear' is a word pointing to something you experience. Let go of the word and let your awareness go to the feeling itself.... Tell me what it's like."

They might say, "It's like standing outside a cave as a wolf emerges from the dark." Or, they might say, "It's like standing on a high cliff in a strong wind." Or they might say, "It's very dark and I don't know where I am."

I respond, "You used the word 'fear' to point to it. Is there a better word for pointing to your actual experience?"

If the person had seen a wolf, they might say, "'Terror' is better." If they were on a high cliff they might say, "Shaky." If they were in the dark they might say, "Alone."

After they settle into this new language, we do the process again: "Set the new pointer aside; see if the feeling relates to some part of the body. Then go back to the underlying experience. Is there a better word?"

Perhaps they find a better word. Or perhaps they return to the same word. The goal of going back and forth from the label to the raw experience is not to get the best label possible. It is to get clear about the distinction between the label and the raw experience itself. We are interested in the moon, not the finger pointing to it. We are interested in the deeper, intuitive sense, not the language.

To get a feel for pointers and underlying experience, try the following:

*Go back to the person, situation, hindrance, or the moment you were exploring before or take a whole new one — whatever seems best to you. Go into your felt sense of it including body sensations, if any.*

*Find a word that points to your experience; let that settle in for a moment....*

*Then let go of the pointer and go back to the raw experience to see if there is a better label....*

*Keep going back and forth until you've found a pointer that best evokes the actual experience.*

This leaves you with a word or pointer that resonates well with your actual experience.

## Deepening

You may have noticed that even if you get a good pointer, often the underlying experience itself morphs. As you come into direct contact with it, awareness itself may cause your experience to deepen into something else.

This natural shifting is what I call "deepening." We let awareness go deeper into the experience and see what happens.

It's as if our experience of fear, joy, anger, or contentment is an energy field. The first part of the process is to find a relatively accurate pointer to that energy field.

The second part is to go into the energetic center of the phenomenon. If it seems like a ball of energy, we go into the middle of the ball and see what's at the center. Some people find it easier to go under that energetic field or behind it. Any of those are fine. The mind does not exist in three-dimensional space, so "going into the center," "going beneath," or "going behind" are just metaphors. Use whatever is most effective for you.

You may remember that the three essential practices of the Buddha are turning toward, relaxing into, and savoring (pp. 52-62). This is what we do in deepening. We turn toward the experience until we have a good enough pointer, relax into the core of it, and then just hang out with whatever we find. If it is an unpleasant feeling, it may not feel like savoring as much as just letting it soak into us or us soak into it. It's all the same.

As we do this, one of three things will happen: (1) nothing changes, (2) the experience intensifies, or (3) something else comes up. For the purposes of this exercise, we don't care which happens. Any of the three is fine. We aren't trying to control the experience. Quite the opposite, we just want to relax into it and let it lead us.

To illustrate this process, consider a more complex example[27]:

*Several years ago, a teacher whom I'll call "Frank" was going to co-lead a meditation group with me. Our teaching styles were different, but he was smart, knowledgeable, and an experienced teacher. Working together could provide a rich tapestry for the yogis.*

*As the class approached, he had an early morning epiphany: he couldn't co-lead with me. He said he didn't want a long conversation about it. But he wanted me to understand his thoughts and wrote a long email.*

*His central concern was that I was not tough enough. Classes provide a rare opportunity to go deeper. He felt it was important to get yogis to work hard. My experience has been that for every meditator who doesn't put in enough effort, there are 20 who put in too much effort. Over-efforting can cause the body and psyche to stiffen. If people back off and let go of the mind's stories, a natural and stable* samādhi *(peacefulness) is likely to emerge. He thought my "easing awake" style would lead to a "pleasant mush," not the clarity and precision of the jhānas.*

*He was also concerned that our different styles would be confusing and give rise to hindrances and discouragement for the yogis. To him, discouraging people from the dhamma was a "mortal sin." This was his tongue-in-cheek way of saying he felt strongly about it.*

*Since he had said he didn't want to discuss it with me, I just sent him a short note: I was disappointed that it wasn't going to work out. However, since he felt working with me would violate his integrity, I understood that he felt he had to withdraw. I wished him well.*

---

[27] This story is essentially true. But to give "Frank" some anonymity, I've altered some of the unessential details.

*I thought my response was clear and accurate, and that it would bring closure.*

*It didn't bring closure. In my next meditation, my mind rumbled. Apparently I was angrier than I'd realized. I ignored the content of the rumbling and used the Six Rs to deepen into the anger itself — relaxed into its very center.*

*It intensified.*

*I kept recognizing, releasing, and relaxing, smiling, and radiating kindness out into the world only to have the mind go into another outburst.*

*I knew from dependent origination, that if awareness got to the subtle conditions underneath, the tension would release. Yet after several days, my mind was still nitpicking and getting more furious. I was stuck. There must've been something I was missing. I opened up more.*

*As I Six-R'd and deepened into the felt sense, I noticed hurt. Deepening into the center of the hurt, there was a softer tenderness. And in the center of the tenderness was loneliness. It seemed ancient and intolerable. But it was clearly there: a deep and familiar aloneness.*

*So I relaxed into the core of the loneliness. A week had gone by now. I was still Six-R'ing, but the mental rumbling and nitpicking had persisted and morphed into loneliness. I let go of the label "loneliness" and sunk into the felt sense of my experience. It was as if I were a piece of bamboo — hard on the outside but hollow, dark, and dusty in the middle.*

*As I let down into that hollowness, a thought trickled up: "Maybe Frank is right. Maybe my practice is mellow mush. Maybe I'm teaching and practicing all wrong."*

*The way my body responded may be surprising: it chuckled and smiled. This was the root condition of the root conditions of the root of the entire episode: I doubted my practice. Worry and doubt come easily to me. The body chuckled more as it resonated with the truth of this. It was such a relief to expose the doubt at the core of my disturbance.*

*Instantly the mind knew exactly what to do. I didn't have to think about it — it was obvious. I'd practice a little harder and notice the effect. Then I'd practice a little softer and notice the effect. I'd conduct an empirical trial. I didn't require anybody — any friend, or any colleague, anyone else — to tell me if my practice was optimal. I'd just experiment and find out directly in my own experience.*

*Suddenly I didn't care what Frank or anyone else thought. I had doubt about my practice and a sure way to find the answer. I almost laughed out loud. And I was grateful to Frank for stimulating some of the causes and conditions that helped this clarity to surface.*

*The body and mind became very deep and peaceful as everything faded but awareness itself. Even that thinned out.*

## Skilled

That story illustrates a way for a monk or lay meditator to be skilled in dependent origination. The art of it is to find the root conditions of suffering and remove them by relaxing into them. We don't try to remove the suffering directly. That would be acting out of aversion. Acting out of disliking sets up more suffering. Instead we look for the root conditions and simply open up and relax into them.

The way to find the root is not to analyze or figure things out. Root causes and conditions are often far subtler than thoughts, concepts, and ideas. The intellect can't go deep enough. But awareness can.

So we set aside our labels and open more directly to the felt sense. As we do, the sense may morph and change. We don't control the morphing and changing. We just follow it until it releases on its own.

## Secret Weapon

Notice that we don't even remove the root conditions. We have a secret weapon to do that for us. It's called "pure awareness." Pure awareness sees things on their own terms without trying to do anything about them. It's not based on controlling or fixing. Our secret weapon is awareness with no agenda.

The German philosopher Martin Heidegger described it this way: imagine an awareness that sees to the heart of suffering with no urge to fix anything. Imagine that this awareness is the opposite of indifference. In other words, imagine an awareness that is deeply engaged and so loving that it has no need to control, change, or fix anything.

That is the kind of awareness the Buddha recommended.

This pure awareness has a magic property. It soothes the mind-heart. As it soothes, tension relaxes. As it relaxes, it clarifies. As it clarifies, insight and wisdom arise in due time.

There is no metaphysical explanation for it. It's just the nature of agendaless awareness. It's like gravity. Why does gravity hold objects to the earth? There is no reason. It's just its nature. It's just what it does. Why does awareness soothe and relax? There is no reason. It's just its nature. It's just what it does.

The trick is to look at what's going on without trying to change it — simple seeing. When we recognize something clearly, the mind releases its grip on it and relaxes. As it relaxes, uplifted qualities flow in and naturally radiate outward. If some tension comes back, the mind patiently repeats the Six Rs.

In other words, to use dependent origination skillfully, we use awareness skillfully. If it doesn't work, it's because awareness is not yet deep or subtle enough — there is probably another condition beneath that felt sense. We don't try to analyze it or figure it out. We let our secret weapon — awareness — look for what we're missing. Attuning to felt sense, distinguishing between pointers and experience, and deepening into what arises gives awareness the space it needs to do its job.

We care for awareness. Then awareness cares for us.

When awareness reaches a root condition, we'll feel it as a release. It might be a little chuckle like mine. It may be just a feeling of relief or ease. Or awareness may just fade into nothingness.

Our job is never to figure things out. It is to invite this pure, guileless, unassuming awareness to see the truth of what's here.

This is how to be skilled in dependent origination.

If you'd like to try it out:

*Close your eyes and see what presents itself....*

*Notice if you feel it in the body. Notice your felt sense of whatever arises.*

*The mind may put a label on it. That's fine. The mind does the labeling on its own. (The labeling is called vicāra in Pāli.) You can let go of the label pointing to the experience and come back to the experience itself....*

*Now, whatever you experience, relax right into the core of it. See what it's like in the center. It may feel the same at the center as it does from a distance. Or it may intensify. Or something else may come up.*

*All these possibilities are fine. We aren't controlling. We're surrendering into awareness.*

*Just follow awareness....*

*If something different comes up, repeat the process and go to its center and see what happens....*

## Corollaries

This process is not how I first learned dependent origination. First, I memorized one of the specific maps of dependent origination. Then I tried to recognize the specific events in my own experience. I wasn't very skilled.

To be skilled in dependent origination, we first learn to feel for the underlying felt sense of whatever our experience is. And to do this we set aside our concepts and labels to go directly into the preverbal experience. It helps to let go and follow that experience with an agendaless awareness, and to allow it to deepen and change naturally on its own.

Once we have that skill, learning some of the traditional maps of dependent origination may help refine our awareness. We'll look at those maps in the next chapter.

But without the skills of felt sense, separating pointers from what's pointed to, and deepening, the maps of dependent origination may be so abstract as to not be so helpful.

The skillful use of dependent origination is allowing a preverbal, precognitive, intuitive awareness to settle into the core of experience without any agenda other than seeing what's there and following the unfolding awareness until the mind, on its own, releases and dissolves.

Here are five corollaries of these practical tools:

## 1: Don't Change Anything

Don't try to change or fix anything. Just sense root conditions with agendaless awareness.

## 2: No Blame

The fact that root conditions are often elusive is not a moral failure. It's a by-product of evolution. Ancestors who honed in on the wolf running across the field toward them were more likely to pass along their DNA than those who fixated on the tree on the edge of the field. We aren't to blame for the laws of evolutionary selection. But we don't have to be limited by those tendencies bred into us.

## 3: Relax

If awareness remains stuck or doesn't release and dissolve, something subtler is going on that awareness has missed. Gently ask, "What am I missing?" Drop the questions, thoughts, ideas, even labels, and open up more to feel any other subtleties. Then relax into those. Be patient. Give awareness the space to do its job.

## 4: Savor

When awareness reaches the root of a causal chain and goes deeply enough into it, the condition will release. We can't force it. But when awareness goes deep enough, we can't resist it either. It may be felt as a laugh, a smile, a sense of well-being, or quiet relief. However it manifests, let it soak in. There's no need to grab hold of it — it's counterproductive to try. However, it is wise to deeply savor a good feeling while it's there. This builds up a reservoir of equanimity. When the next burning match, insult, or bad news comes along, that reservoir serves as a shock absorber. We are less reactive. Our peace becomes more stable.

## 5: Tenderness and Spaciousness

Underneath hurt there is always tenderness — without tenderness, there is no hurt. Underneath the tenderness is spaciousness — without spaciousness there is no tenderness. If we want more spaciousness and the wisdom and clarity that comes with it, the fastest route is not to run from our experience but to deepen into it until the natural, underlying vastness of the impersonal mind-heart is exposed. (This model is also explored on pp. 39-42 and pp. 51-52.)

# 9

# *Holding Dear*

The Buddha was interested in how *dukkha* (suffering) happens. So he reverse-engineered his own suffering by carefully observing how it worked. He saw that his experience of difficulty was preceded by some kind of action. It might have been as obvious as physical or verbal action or as subtle as mental action, resistance, or identification. That action or identification was shaped by a habitual tendency. The habit pattern, in turn, had been preceded by thought. The thought had been preceded by a preverbal liking, disliking, or confusion. And so on down the line like a string of dominos (see p. 118). He reverse-engineered the suffering until he understood how it emerged.

Usually we reverse-engineer a widget so we can produce our own widget. But the Buddha was not interested in learning how to produce misery. We humans seem to be pretty good at that already. He wanted to understand how bummers arose so he could stop them from arising. He wanted to know how to keep one of those dominos from falling over, or how to take one out of the line, or how to spread them far enough apart so that one might fall without knocking over the next. If he understood the causal sequence, he might be able to shut it down.

And he did. It worked. He woke up and became fully liberated. The Buddha solved his problem.

But that doesn't solve ours.

We must reverse-engineer our own angst and dissatisfaction because suffering is internal. There can be external events in our causal chain, but the suffering at the end of the line is subjective. The Buddha's descriptions of the inner events are only approximations. They may not match our experience exactly. To solve our problem, we have to understand our difficulty in more detail than anyone can convey to us. If we look openly, deeply, kindly, and directly inside, all we need to know is right there. But we can only come to know it intimately by observing our own processes. To unplug our suffering, we have to reverse-engineer it enough to understand our own causal chain.

# Dependent Origination

The Buddha's sequence became known as *paṭiccasamuppāda* (dependent origination or dependent co-arising), and the individual elements in the sequence became known as *niḍāna* or "links." (See "The Paradox of Paticcasamuppāda" pp. 157-160 for a discussion of niḍāna and paṭiccasamuppāda.)

In the previous chapter, we explored the nature of the causes and conditions that make up a link. To use dependent origination as a practical tool, we must learn to see and release the conditions that give rise to angst. Many tools can help. We looked at a few: felt sense, pointers, and deepening.

Once we can see and release the subtle conditions within us, the Buddha's maps of dependent origination are less like philosophical exercises and more like tools for awareness. As we become facile with these tools and awarenesses, the Buddha's particular maps of dependent origination offer encouragement and pointers as to where we can look next as we reverse-engineer our own patterns.

We have to reverse-engineer our own experience because it's a little different for each of us. However, we are all human. There are

> **Niḍāna** is a Pāli term that is a synonym for *hetupaccayo* ("causes conditions" see p. 118). However it is usually translated as "link" when referring to dependent origination because it links adjacent elements. It is also sometimes translated as "cause" or "condition."

general patterns of dependent origination that we all share. Understanding these patterns can help us discover our own unique expressions and variations.

The Buddha offered several versions of dependent origination. Perhaps the most widely known is called "The twelve links of dependent origination." We find it scattered throughout the *Majjhima Nikāya*, the *Samyutta Nikāya*, and other collections of suttas. It is summarized on the right side of the table on page 142.

This schema was first recorded two or three centuries after the Buddha died and finalized several centuries later. Prior to being transcribed, it had been passed down orally from monk to monk for generations. During this transmission, it was codified to make it easier to memorize. The same codification can make it mind-numbing to follow.

An earlier version is found in a collection of 16 suttas called the *Atthaka Vagga*. This collection is the oldest known record we have of the Buddha's teachings. It was probably written down during his lifetime. It comes closer to what he actually said than the *Majjhima* and *Samyutta Nikāyas*. It is summarized on the left side of the table on page 143.

In the *Atthaka Vagga*, the Buddha is not referred to as "Lord Buddha" or "The Blessed One." He's simply "the Wanderer," or "Sir Gautama." It's early in his ministry. There is no *sangha* yet — it would gather as the years passed. Still, he was charismatic and deeply respected as he struggled to find words to express his extraordinary experience. These suttas have no Eightfold Path, Four Ennobling Truths, five hindrances, three characteristics, twelve links, or numbered anything. They're just informal dialogs.

The eleventh sutta of the *Atthaka Vagga* is called "Quarrels and Disputes." It can be found in *Sutta Nipata* 4.11. It contains what scholars consider the earliest record of dependent origination. The Buddha doesn't even use the term "paṭiccasamuppāda." Nevertheless he lays out a string of causal relationships in response to a series of questions.

The sutta is short. I'll go through it line by line with only a few comments. Then I'll unpack its elements in more detail.

# In the Buddha's Words[28]

The sutta opens with a question posed to the Buddha:

*Where do quarrels and disputes* (kalahā vivādā) *come from? And sorrow, grief, and selfishness? And the pride, arrogance, insults, and lies that come with them? Why do they happen? Please tell me.*

Notice that *dukkha* (suffering) is described as quarrels and disputes, rather than birth, aging, sickness, death, and so on in the later versions. It's the same idea, but the images are closer to everyday life. The later versions were not written down until hundreds of years after the Buddha died. They are probably less true to what the Buddha intended.

The Buddha answers:

*Disputes and quarrels come from what we hold dear (piya). Sorrow, grief, and selfishness, pride, arrogance, and slander come with them. When we argue we speak spitefully. Selfishness is yoked to quarrels and disputes.*

He says *dukkha* comes from holding dear (*piya*). In the later suttas it's called clinging (*upādāna*). It's the same idea, but the early text is less accusatory. We hold our children dear, and they do cause us suffering. But we wouldn't trade them in or fault ourselves for caring about them. However, we might fault ourselves for clinging. In using "holding dear," the Buddha wasn't passing moral judgment. He was just describing how it works. The moralistic tone of the later text is probably more reflective of the community of monks or broader culture than the Buddha himself.

The questioner asks:

---

[28] This rendering was compiled from translations by Leigh Brasington, Ajahn Buddhadāsa, John D. Ireland, K. R. Norman, Andrew Olendzki, Santikaro, Thanissaro Bhikkhu, and by Lesley Fowler Lebkowicz, Tamma Ditrich, and Primoz Pecenko. Leigh Brasington has a table of several translations on his website (http://www.leighb.com).

*Where does this endearing (piyāsu) come from? Why do we feel the longing and greed that go with it? What creates hopes and aspirations?*

The Buddha responds:

*Endearing comes from desire (chanda) — we want things. Greed is part of the worldly life. It causes hopes and aspirations for the future.*

Endearing comes from desire or longing (*chanda*). In the later texts it's called craving (*taṇhā*). It's the same idea, but less moralistic. Again, the Buddha is not judging, just describing what happens.

Question:

*Where does desire (chanda) come from? And what about preferences, anger, lies, doubt, and all the states the Wanderer talks about?*

The wandering Buddha responds:

*Desire (chanda) comes from what we call "pleasing" and "unpleasing" (sātam asātanti). Likewise, when people see how things come and go, they form preferences accordingly.*

*Anger, lies, doubt, and confusion follow. We're bound by the duality of pleasing and unpleasing. If you doubt this, train yourself to know it. You'll understand when you've seen what these states are like.*

The words "pleasing" and "unpleasing" (*sātam asātanti*) become "feeling tone" (vedanā) in the later suttas. Vedanā means pleasant, painful, or something that's neither pleasant nor painful, as we saw in chapter 6 (pp. 89-92). It's the same idea as *sāta asātanti*.

Question:

*Where does the feeling of pleasing or unpleasing come from? When are these states absent? What makes them come and go? Please tell me.*

The Buddha:

*Pleasing and unpleasing come from sense impressions (phassa). Without sense impressions, they don't occur. The same happens with coming and going — they come from sense impressions.*

The word for "sense impression" is *phassa*. Phassa is often translated as "contact." It means raw sensation without interpretation (see pp. 75 and 80).

Question:

*So where in this world do sense impressions come from? Why do we grasp things? What must be absent for this selfishness to fade? What needs to be gone, for sense impressions to disappear?*

The Buddha:

*Body-mind depends upon sense impressions. Grasping things comes from calling them "mine." When there is no desire, there is no sense of self. When body-mind is gone, there are no sense impressions.*

In other words, if you want to get rid of sense impressions and the selfishness and desire that come with them, get rid of the body-mind. That's probably not going to happen!

A nicer way to say this is that the tendencies toward grasping and believing in a personal self arise out of the body-mind itself. The forces of evolution favored those who had a fierce instinct to protect the integrity of the body. Those who were lackadaisical about keeping the body going were eaten and their DNA was taken out of the gene pool. There is no self that creates this instinct any more than there is a self that causes the knee-jerk reflex. It's a byproduct of our genetic inheritance. It just emerges from natural body-mind processes.

Question:

*What do we have to do for sense impressions to disappear? For happiness and unhappiness to cease? Tell us please, we really want to know.*

The Buddha:

*Neither perceiving, misperceiving, nor non-perceiving — in this state, mind-body vanishes from awareness. Conceptualizing is where the problem starts. Conceptualizing is also the cause of incessant thinking.*

Perception involves conceptualization, if only to put a label on an experience (see pp. 76-78). As the mind gets deeply relaxed, conceptualizing fades naturally.

Remember that in dependent origination, the dominos get smaller and subtler as we move up the causal chain (see p. 118). The Buddha describes a state where there is neither perception, misperception, nor non-perception. It is indeed very subtle. But as we settle deeper into the jhānas, we experience it.

Question:

*Whatever we have asked, you've revealed to us. Another question, please. Do all the wise men say this is the highest purity? Or is there something higher?*

In other words, is neither perception nor non-perception the highest we can attain? The Buddha answers:

*Some wise men say this is the highest. And some speak of a state where nothing remains. A genuine sage knows how everything is conditioned. Understanding conditioning, he is free and content. Knowing better, he does not dispute. The wise do not keep becoming.*

"Understanding conditioning" means understanding dependent origination. To "not keep becoming" means to wake up.

The implication is that there is nothing but a stream of conditioned phenomena that flow on and on. There is no self-essence behind it, just changing experience. There is no permanent self, just fluctuating phenomenon. When we fully understand that, we are free. Phenomena flow on, but there's no longer the sense of an independent self caught in the chain of events. If there is no one to suffer, there is no suffering.

Notice this is not a theological, philosophical, or metaphysical claim. It is just an experience. Hence there is nothing to dispute. The sutta ends by returning to the original question about quarrels and disputes. The wise don't engage in them.

Leigh Brasington is a scholar with a mature meditation practice. He comments on this sutta:

*These verses, rather than feeling like the record of an actual conversation, have the feeling of being intentionally composed — the questions are just too perfect, with each set of questions having a single answer. But this does not detract at all from the significance of this sutta — it is clearly a well thought out discourse describing a series of "necessary conditions." This is the links of Dependent Origination [or Dependent Co-arising] in their earliest form. It would seem that any explanation of links of Dependent Origination ought to harmonize with this early description if the later description is going to be accurate. This is as close as we can get to the Gold Standard for understanding the Buddha's original thinking about Dependent Origination. And given what the Buddha says…, understanding his early thinking on Dependent Origination is a requirement for awakening.*[29]

# Unpacking

Notice that the sutta begins with the "big dominos" of coarse suffering (quarrels, disputes, and other obvious discomfort). It traces the origin of this and subsequent links to smaller and subtler "little dominos." This is the order in which we are likely to encounter the various links in our experience. And it is the order in which we can most easily defuse them.

However, to understand the full flow of dependent origination, it may be helpful to trace the links in the opposite direction — that is, start with the subtle phenomena and follow each link up to the big dominos of full-blown misery. I'll describe the links in this order starting with sense impressions. As I trace them from subtle to coarse phenomena, I'll compare the language in the early and later texts (see the table summary), and I'll bring in some of the insights of evolutionary psychology and neural science that I described in earlier chapters (pp. 70-82).

## Raw Sense Impressions: Phassa

The smallest dominos can be difficult to recognize without meditation training. But all of us can recognize sense impression. For example, you hear a sound. Before you identify it as the rumbling of distant traffic or peepers in the pond, there is the raw sensation of the sound itself with no interpretation. Or perhaps you feel heat. For a moment you don't know the source or its name. There is just warmth.

Those are raw sensory impressions (*phassa*). They are unadorned, unlabeled, unconceptualized sensations: light, sound,

---

[29] More of Leigh Brasington's commentary can be found on his website at http://www.leighb.com/snp4_11.htm.

taste, smell, touch, or mind objects. We have no control over them. They arise from the contact between a sensory energy (such as sound), a sensory organ (such as an ear) and a sensory awareness (such as hearing).

| Phases of *Paṭiccasamuppāda* | | | |
|---|---|---|---|
| Dependent Origination as presented in the early and later suttas. | | | |
| **Early Text:** | | **Late Text:** | |
| ***Sutta Nipata 4.11*** | | ***Majjhima Nikāya 115*** | |
| Pāli | English | Pāli | English |
| *Kalahā & vivādā* | Quarrels & disputes: sorrow, grief, selfishness, pride, arrogance, insults, lies, arrogance, slander | *Jarā & maraṇa* | Aging & death; sorrow, lamentation, pain, grief, despair |
| | | *Jāti* | Birth of action |
| | | *Bhava* | Habitual tendencies |
| *Piya* | Holding dear, endearing | *Upādāna* | Clinging |
| *Chanda* | Desire | *Taṇhā* | Craving |
| *Sātam asātanti* | Pleasing/displeasing | *Vedanā* | Feeling tone: pleasant, unpleasant, neutral |
| *Phassa* | Contact, sense impression | *Phassa* | Contact, sense impression |
| *Nāmarūpa* | Mind-body | *Āyatana* | Six sense bases |
| | | *Nāmarūpa* | Mind-body |
| *Na visaññasaññi* | Neither perceiving nor non-perceiving | *Viññāṇa* | Consciousness |
| | | *Saṅkhāra* | Formations |
| | | *Avijjā* | Ignorance |

### Signal, Feeling Tone: Sātam Asātanti, Vedanā

Raw sensation can give rise to a signal that says, "Pay more attention to this." In the early text, the signal is called "pleasing/unpleasing" (*sātam asātanti*). In the later text, it's called "feeling tone" (*vedanā*), which can be pleasant, painful, or neither. They are the same idea.

Sātam asātanti/vedanā is like a light on the dashboard or the movement of the needle on a dial. It's not an alarm bell, flashing light, or an exclamation like "Fire!" It's an unemotional, uncharged indicator of a safety need ("That could be a threat"), satisfaction need ("That could satisfy my hunger"), or a connection need ("That person looks nice").

It is neither verbal nor cognitive. It's a wordless impression. If the signal is about a threat, it feels uncomfortable. If it's about a need satisfaction, it feels pleasing or pleasant. If it's about connection, it feels like a draw to move closer to the person or a push to move away. And if the signal is about something for which we don't have enough information, it feels dull, thick, or unclear and without a valence — neither pleasant nor painful (pp. 89-92).

Pain, pleasantness, and lack of clarity get bad press in spiritual circles. But they are just signals. Without them, we couldn't live.[30] Without them, we'd walk in front of busses, forget to eat, get bitten by dogs, walk barefoot in the snow, and not bother to get out of bed in the morning. To survive without these signals, our minds would be consumed by intellectually puzzling out the relevance of every little sensation.

We depend on *satam asātanti/vedanā* to preprocess information and send signals if something needs attention.

Remember: the vedanā signal has very little charge. It's possible to enjoy ice cream, know that it's pleasant, but feel no need for more. Similarly, something can be uncomfortable without aversion. Perhaps we stubbed our toe. For a split second we noticed, "Oh, I may have damaged it. I think this is going to hurt." A second later the pain hits: "Ow! I don't like this!" But for a short moment, there was awareness without aversion — a quiet signal that something happened.

### Charge: Chanda, Taṇhā

The signal itself can be so laid back and unobtrusive that we ignore it. Theoretically we could back into a hot stove, overlook a rattlesnake by the path, or walk past good food without noticing. So

---

[30] For a longer discussion of this point, see Doug Kraft, "Unhealthy Desire vs. Healthy Wisdom," *Meditator's Field Guide.*

we have a backup mechanism that grabs our attention by energizing our system. It jacks up our motivation to do something.

If the signal is about a threat, the charge might be aversion, hatred, dislike, anger, or "let's get outta here." If the signal is about need satisfaction, the charge might be attraction, liking, lust, craving, greed, or yearning. If the signal is neither pleasant nor painful, the charge could be confusion, ignorance, or curiosity.

If the charge is clear, wise, and impersonal, it's called "wholesome desire" (*chanda*). If it's cloudy, distorted, or personalized, it's called "unwholesome desire" (*taṇhā*.) Both are what psychologists call "drive states." The good news is they can push us to act when it's wise. The bad news is they can distort our perception so that we act unwisely.

## Holding Dear and Clinging: Piya and Upādāna

Up to this point, there are no words or concepts. *Chanda* and *taṇhā* are a preverbal, preconceptual tightening. A sensation (*phassa*) has produced a signal (*sātam asātanti, vedanā*) that has produced a tension (*chanda, taṇhā*) to do something about something. But we don't know what to do.

The next phase of dependent origination sets us up to figure out what to do. If the charge is not relaxed, the mind shrink-wraps around it and cloaks it in a thought. The thought might be a label, word, or image. This is called "holding dear" (*piya*) in the early text and "clinging" (*upādāna*) in the later text. Holding dear / clinging is always experienced as a thought.

This is where a sense of self sends down roots. The feeling of pushing / pulling or endearing / unendearing gives rise to a sense of an object we like or don't like and a self who likes or dislikes.

This is also where suffering begins. In the early and later texts, suffering is said to arise from any experience "affected by clinging (or holding dear)." When asked why we suffer, the Burmese meditation master U Tejaniya said, "We need the motivation." *Piya* and *upādāna* give us the motivation.

## Habitual Tendencies, Becoming: Bhāva

Now we have an urge to act and a focus on something to be dealt with. But we don't have a plan. The plan is created by the next phase. It is called *bhāva*, or "habitual tendencies" or "becoming."

*Bhāva* is our collection of beliefs, ideas, emotional tendencies, intellectual dispositions, and leanings. We tend to identify with these, so bhāva is often translated as "becoming." The thought created by our endearing or clinging is thrown into all our tendencies. They devise a strategy. This is not always done consciously or wisely. But an action plan is formed.

## Birth of Action: Jāti

If executed, our plan gives birth to action (*jāti*). The action might be physical (we do something), verbal (we say something), or mental (we think something or form an opinion). All of these qualify as "birth of action" or simply "action."

In the early text, habitual tendencies and action are nested into *piya* (endearing). In the later text, they are separated into different links.

The Buddha said the weak link in dependent origination is the charge of *chanda/taṇhā* – the preverbal, preconceptual tightening. If we can feel it and relax, then the clinging/endearing, habitual tendencies, action, and suffering are cut off at the source. There is nothing to fuel them.

Dependent origination was meant to be a practical meditation tool, not a philosophical treatise. The simpler early text gives us what we need to relax the tension and find contentment. As the text was transmitted through many generations of monks, it probably became more complex in structure and moralistic in tone. This simple freedom of the Buddha's original language may better reflect what he cared about most: a deep contentment with life as it is.

If we relax the grip of holding dear, then the tendency toward suffering ceases. If we don't, then it may quickly lead to suffering.

## Quarrels, Disputes, and Suffering: Kalahā, Vivādā, and Jarāmaraṇa

We noted (on p. 138) that *dukkha* (suffering) is described as quarrels and disputes (*kalahā vivādā*) in the early text. It's a topic we can imagine being discussed around the kitchen table or on the front porch. In the later text, the issue is elevated out of the daily context into the grandiose symbols of aging and death (*jarāmaraṇa*). This is typical of the difference between the early and later texts. The early is more concerned with the practical, everyday stresses while the later text feels like a treatise discussed in a graduate philosophy seminar. The early text is probably closer to the Buddha while the later is closer to the Buddhist monks several centuries after the Buddha's death.

However, it's clear in both texts that the Buddha was referring to many kinds of gross and subtle angst, including but not limited to the ones he mentioned: quarrels, disputes, sorrow, selfishness, pride, arrogance, insults, lies, slander, aging, death, lamentation, pain, grief, and despair.

# Practical

On the first day of class, my college biology professor said, "Your high school biology was probably a large vocabulary test where you spent most of the time learning the names of various organs. In this class we're more interested in how things work than in what you call them. But you'll be tested on both."

The strength of dependent origination is giving an appreciation for the breadth and complexity of our experience. The weakness is that we can get so caught up in the labels and language that the fluidity of awareness gets replaced by a bunch of Pāli terms, particularly if we hold those terms dear.

In the last chapter (pp. 123-129), we looked at some practical, non-labeling tools to work with the flow of evolving awareness. I'd like to offer a few more tools. But before we get to those, it may help to go through my meditation experience after Frank withdrew from co-leading the group with me (described on pp. 127-129). This time I'll add in the Pāli terms. I hope this will help take the Pāli terms out of a conceptual box. They are just pointers to fluctuating conditions.

# Meditation

*The day after Frank withdrew from co-leading the group, I got up to meditate early the next morning. I began with my usual practice of radiating equanimity. Very quickly, the mind was pulled away by rumbling in the background. It didn't feel so good. This was jarāmaraṇa, the final link of the twelve links of dependent origination that appears in* Majjhima Nikāya 115. *It's called "kalahā vivādā" ("quarrels and disputes") in the earlier* Sutta Nipata 4.11. *The terms allude to a variety of discomforts from the gross to the subtle.*

*So I Six-R'd the rumbling: recognized, released, relaxed, re-smiled, and returned to sending out equanimity. Pretty soon, rumbling pulled the mind away again. I Six-R'd. The rumbling popped back up. I Six-R'd when needed. And so on.*

*I noticed that within the rumbling, the mind was nitpicking fights with Frank. I Six-R'd the nitpicking before it turned into generalized grumbling.*

*The nitpicking was jāti in the later text of the* Majjhima Nikāya. *In this case it was mental action. Or it could also be considered verbal action — dialog inside the mind. It was one of the causes of the rumbling. In the earlier* Sutta Nipata, *this is not listed as a separate link — it's part of kalahā vivādā, "quarrels and disputes."*

*As I Six-R'd the jāti, I could feel within it an old tendency of my mind to explain things. In the* Majjhima Nikāya, *this is called "bhāva" or "habitual tendencies." In the earlier* Sutta Nipata, *it's part of quarrels and disputes.*

*As I became better at recognizing my old habit, I Six-R'd it before the habitual tendency turned into nitpicking. As I was catching these links earlier and earlier, I was able to sit a little bit longer before the mind was dragged into the drama. And I was relaxing out of the drama a little sooner.*

*Seeing this process more clearly, I started to notice several phrases or ideas that elicited the explaining tendency: "mellow mush," "not tough enough," or "not good enough." These labels were much simpler than the actions or habitual tendencies they caused. This is upādāna or "clinging" in the* Majjhima Nikāya. *The mind shrink-wrapped and clung to a word or phrase. In the earlier text it's piya, "cherishing" or "holding dear." It may seem counterintuitive to call this "cherishing" or "holding dear" because of its negative qualities. However, we can cherish or endear something negative — it happens all the time. Sometimes I call this "thingifying" — the mind turns a flow of experience into a thing. It reifies a movement into a solid concept that the habitual tendencies weave into a story or a mental construct.*

*I Six-R'd the clinging or holding dear before it could set off the explaining and nitpicking.*

*There was quite a charge within the words "mellow mush" or "not tough enough." As I Six-R'd and relaxed into the thingifying, the charge became clearer and clearer. I could see it and Six-R before the mind shrink-wrapped around the word or phrase. Words and phrases are verbal. The charge is preverbal. I can put a label on it, but it's a finger pointing to the moon — it's not the actual experience.*

*So I set the labels and concepts aside. That's when I began to feel anger. Anger is an aversive charge. It's a form of taṇhā or craving. In the earlier text it's called chanda, which means desire but has a less negative valence. But in this case the charge did feel negative.*

*Beneath the anger was a less charged vedanā — emotionally painful vedanā. Painful vedanā arises in response to a threat to the system. Obviously, my system had felt threatened by Frank's critique. In the early text, it's called* sātam asātanti, *which means pleasant or unpleasant. It's the same idea as vedanā, but slightly different language.*

*As I Six-R'd the anger and deepened into it, a different flavor of taṇhā arose: hurt. As I deepened into the hurt, another flavor of taṇhā arose: a hollow loneliness. As awareness deepened into the center of the loneliness, it felt tender. I felt how I was holding back — I had resisted the notion that I might be doing something wrong. I felt vulnerability and doubt — again different flavors of taṇhā and vedanā.*

*While conceptually tenderness and doubt may sound terrible, it was such a relief. It resonated deeply with all I'd been feeling. It all came into focus. I had doubted my system's own wisdom, thinking maybe he'd been right. Doubt is another flavor of vedanā or sātam asātanti.*

*This may have been a blow to my ego construct and self-identity (bhāva or habitual tendency). But the clear awareness just softened and released it.*

*It was such a relief, the body laughed quietly in delight. "Oh yeah, that's what's going on."*

*Once I could see that clearly, it was no longer a big deal. The mind knew what to do with that. It wasn't really a problem. The tension drained out of the system in the presence of the clear, nonjudgmental, agendaless awareness. And the natural equanimity of the mind was exposed as the suffering released.*

*This was the beginning of just nāmarūpa — mind-heart-body without a charge.*

I hope that inserting the names of the traditional links (*niḍāna*) into the story illuminates the kinds of experiences the links point to. And I hope it's clear that names are only names. Our actual experience rarely fits a mold. The map is not the territory. A map helps guide our inward exploration, but it is only a guide. It can't tell us precisely what we'll find. It's up to us to do the actual looking.

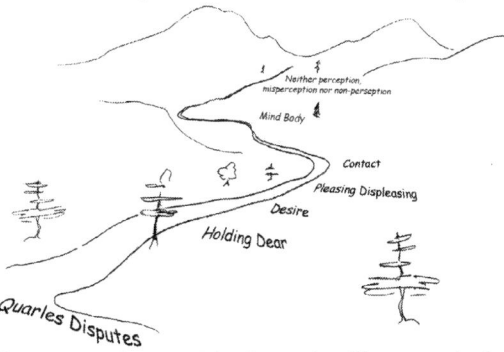

The table (on p. 143) may make the various links look like discreet events, each in a separate box. But our actual experience is more like a river: it's a flow of energy that changes. There is a big difference between the rapids, waterfalls, deep gorges, and quiet meandering sections of the river. However, the various factors are somewhat arbitrary markers along a continuum. In the earliest text,

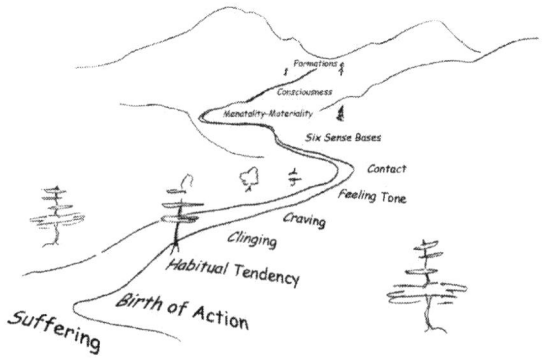

the Buddha describes
seven factors. In later
texts he describes 10,
12, 13, and even 42.
The deepening
process described in
the last chapter (pp.
126-129) doesn't
predefine any labels
other than "pointers" and "felt sense." Yet in all these, the river of
our experience is the same.

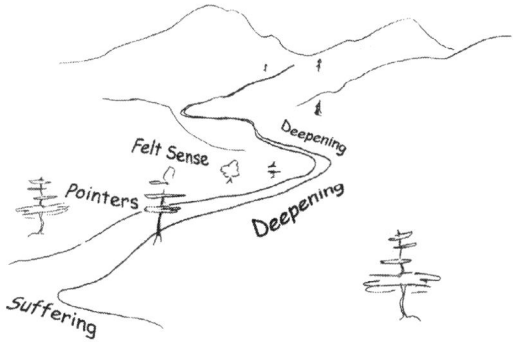

The river, of course, is just a metaphor. While it may be helpful
to get a feel for the various phases of the river, it's best to let our
experience be fluid rather than tightly defined. The energy in our
lives flows from one thing to another rather than making quantum
leaps. And we rarely flow in one direction for very long: we are
constantly moving up and down the river.

Another metaphor for dependent origination is
nesting Russian dolls. Each doll contains within
it the subtler energies that gave rise
to it (as we found with the
deepening process, pp. 126-
129). When we're caught in a
habitual pattern, we can look
for the subtler clinging/holding dear and the tension within it. They
aren't just in the past. They are right here inside the habitual pattern,
like a doll within a doll.

Regardless of what map or metaphor we use, once we know the
experience, we may not need the map because we can see the causal
relationships directly. In the "Greater Discourse on the Destruction
of Craving" ("Mahātaṇhāsankhaya Sutta," *Majjhima Nikāya* 38.14),
the Buddha uses his famous metaphor of the raft. We don't want to
hop off the raft in the middle of the river. However:

> *Monks, purified and bright as this [dependent origination] is, if you*
> *adhere to it, cherish it, treasure it, and treat it as a possession, you*

*would not truly understand the Dhamma. It is similar to a raft, being for the purpose of crossing over, not for the purpose of grasping.*

The point of dependent origination is not to become an expert at paddling up and down the river. It is to gain enough mastery to reach the far shore and leave the raft behind. It is to open the last Russian doll and see that it is empty. We hold no more because there is nothing to hold.

This is the freedom of the open heart.

# Corollaries

Dependent origination has many corollaries for how we practice and how we live. In the previous chapter (pp. 131-132) I mentioned five: (1) not trying to fix or change ourselves but simply seeing our root conditioning more clearly; (2) not blaming ourselves for tendencies bred into us by evolutionary selection; (3) relaxing or softening; (4) savoring or letting subtle awareness soak in until tension releases; and (5) using our tenderness as a gateway to spaciousness.

To these five we can add 6 through 10:

### 6: Subtle Causes, Not Effects

Work with the causes of phenomena rather than the phenomena themselves. In Buddhism, *wisdom* means seeing dependent origination. And seeing dependent origination means seeing these causal relationships. So if we want peace and compassion in our lives and we try to force peace and compassion, we'll be acting out of desire or aversion. Those are not wholesome qualities. We'll be reinforcing unwholesomeness of forcing or pushing.

On the other hand, relaxing into our experience is part of the root cause of peace and compassion. As awareness grows it has a calming effect on the mind.

There can be many causes and conditions that contribute to one event. But we relax and notice the subtler causes underneath or within. These are key. If we relax the originating causes, the results disappear.

### 7: Six-R'ing to Reveal Dependent Origination

Six-R'ing (*aka* wise effort) reveals root causes and conditions. The meditation practice the Buddha taught was designed to help us see dependent origination more clearly.

### 8: Don't Control Thought — Release Tension

It doesn't help to try to stop thoughts. They don't appear until the holding dear/clinging link. Their root cause is the energy of *chanda/taṇhā*. That charge is always experienced as preverbal tension or tightness. If we recognize, release, and relax that tension, verbal thoughts will not arise. Or if they have already arisen, they will fade away because we've removed the root cause.

On the other hand, directly trying to get rid of thoughts just puts more charge, tension, and tightness into our system. That will give rise to more holding dear/clinging. And with that, more thoughts.

### 9: Stability Without Concentration

Notice that in the example about my meditation experience, after Frank declined to co-lead the group, my mind-heart became very serene, stable, and mindful. But I didn't actually create that state. All I did was release the tension pointed out by the distractions. As we release tightness, the mind-heart finds its natural collectedness. Mindfulness becomes bright and clear by itself. And it is wide open rather than focused on a single object. Yet it is remarkably stable.

### 10: No Wheel

There is no wheel or circle in dependent origination, despite all the traditional iconography. The Buddha never used those metaphors. They are a conflation of dependent origination with the wheel of saṃsāra.

Dependent origination is a one-directional flow. Suffering does not flow back into the ignorance that started the whole thing. In fact, with wise practice, suffering can start a flow toward enlightenment. But that's another story.

# Holding in Our Hearts

Before leaving the topic of holding dear, let's step back from the corollaries to the main point. The punchline of the Buddha's earliest teaching on dependent origination is that suffering arises from holding something in our heart — from holding onto what we find precious in life. This seems to suggest that the road to happiness is to become so detached and indifferent that nothing matters. However, that is a formula for depression. Pushing life away is aversion and a form of suffering.

So the Buddha recommended cultivating dispassion. Dispassion means having an interest in life without attaching to any particular outcome. We remain attentive but don't get hooked. Rather than close ourselves off, we open our eyes and hearts wide to see life as it really is and see it without preference. Life becomes alive, vibrant, peaceful, and completely impersonal.

The laws of dependent origination were the Buddha's way of describing in detail how dispassion works and how it can be cultivated. Like the law of gravity, the laws of causation affect us all and remain impersonal.

The *Udāna* (8.8) tells a story about the difference between indifference and dispassion:

*Visākhā went to the Buddha with wet hair and wet garments. She was beside herself with grief because her granddaughter had died. The Buddha knew she had many children and grandchildren. He asked if she would like to have as many descendants as there were people in Sāvatthī, the small city where she lived.*

*She said she'd like that very much.*

*The Buddha asked how many people die every day in Sāvatthī.*

*"Many," she said.*

*The Buddha reminded her that her granddaughter's death was not unusual. People died every day. It was natural. If she had as many children as there were people in the city, she'd be grieving all the time. The Buddha concluded: "The sorrows, lamentations, the many kinds of suffering in the* world, exist dependent on something held dear. They don't exist when there's nothing held dear."

In this poignant teaching moment, the Buddha impressed on her the cause and effect relationship between holding someone dear and suffering.

But I don't think he was recommending ridding ourselves of loved ones or closing our hearts. His point was the opposite. He recommended that we love mightily but not get hooked; open our hearts to the world but remember that everything we love will vanish. He recommended dispassion but not disinterest.

We can't will ourselves into dispassion. It cannot be done with stern resolve. It can only be cultivated by softening and opening as we look with clear eyes at how the world truly is. The Buddha encourages us to mature beyond our evolutionary tendencies toward defending or running away — fight or flight. He encourages us to stay steadfastly with things as they truly are.

That means holding loved ones in our hearts but not holding onto them. There's another ancient story about this that speaks to the Buddha's point.

# It's Already Broken

*A student came to his teacher mourning the loss of a dear friend. He asked, "How can I find peace in this life, knowing that everything I hold dear will be taken from me?"*

*The teacher smiled and lifted a glass. He said, "This lovely goblet was given to me by a dear student. I can hold it up, and lovely patterns of sunlight flow through it. It is beautiful. But I know this glass is already broken. It's just a matter of time. I know this deep in my heart.*

*"You don't accept this. So you try to protect the glass, lock it up safely in a cupboard where you can't enjoy it. For you it becomes an object of fear and protection.*

*"But it doesn't matter. Someday the cat may knock it off the shelf or some other accident will happen. It is inevitable.*

*"So rather than try to escape what is impossible to avoid, I enjoy it while it's here. I savor it because my time with it is precious and fleeting.*

*"And when it breaks, I'll say 'Of course.'"*

*"When you train yourself to know that everything is already broken, rather than shrinking into the shadows, your heart opens widely."*

## Two Reflections

I close with two reflections:

*1. What do you hold most dear? What people, ideas, things, values are important to you?*

*2. How do you hold what is most dear? Do you love because you want something back? Do you care because you want care in return? Are you kind in order to make people kinder to you? Do you treat kindness like a monetary exchange — a means to an end? Or are love, care, and kindness ends in and of themselves?*

When we see that the glass is already broken, that all relationships will end someday, then we stay open just for the sake of love, caring, and kindness. Then we are free. At first, freedom may have a bittersweet poignancy. But it is the path to true liberation, bound by nothing, eyes clear, and heart open to the winds of change.

# 10

# The Paradox of
# Paticcasamuppāda

In the previous two chapters, we explored *paṭiccasamuppāda* (dependent origination) and ways it can guide us toward alleviating suffering. Before we leave this topic, I'd like to turn back to the word itself to explore a few of its nuances. The variety of ways it has been translated suggest some of its subtlety, complexity, and paradoxical nature.

The term is composed of several Pāli words. Each of these words has several meanings:

*pattica*: grounded on, dependent on, cause, condition, because of, concerning

*sama*: similar, same, equal

*uppāda*: arise, exist

When these three are combined, the "a" at the end of "sama" is removed to make it more pronounceable. The resulting compound word is "paṭiccasamuppāda." It has been rendered into English in many ways including:

dependent origination

dependent arising

interdependent co-arising

conditional co-arising

All of these renderings have merit even though some seem to contradict others. How can something depend on a preceding cause and also co-arise with it? We have to look a little deeper to sort this out.

# Niḍāna

Paṭiccasamuppāda is described as a series of internal events, each of which arises out of antecedent causes and conditions and is itself the cause or condition of a subsequent event. It is like a string of falling dominos in which one falls, knocking over the next, which knocks over the next, and so on (see p. 118). The sequence ends in suffering or dissatisfaction.

However, the individual events are called *niḍāna,* which means "link." Notice the sleight of hand in this label; it suggests there are no events that are linked together. Rather, each event *is* a link and each link *is* the event itself. How can that be?

An analogy may offer the best clue. Imagine snowmelt from an Alpine field trickling into a brook that slips over a waterfall that splashes into a stream that meanders into a lake that flows into a river that merges with the ocean. There are obvious and apparent differences between snowmelt, brooks, waterfalls, streams, lakes, rivers, and oceans. Yet the essence of each is the same: simple water. This essence manifests in different forms depending on the conditions around it.

In a similar way, paṭiccasamuppāda flows from one link/event to another as each takes a different shape. Yet the underlying essence is the same in all of them.

# Tanhā

It is easy to overlook one of the essential properties of water: cohesion. Liquid water tends to stick to itself even as it takes different shapes in its flow from a trickle to the ocean. If the cohesion is lost, the water evaporates and all those forms disappear. The water remains suspended invisibly in the air. But there is no longer a stream, a lake, or a river.

In a similar way, it is easy to overlook one of the essential properties of paṭiccasamuppāda: *taṇhā* (tension or tightness). Though not explicit in the name, taṇhā is key to understanding how tightly the elements of dependent origination can be tied together. Taṇhā is the fuel that moves paṭiccasamuppāda from one element to the next.

For example, I can eat a macaroon, find it pleasurable, tighten around that pleasantness, and desire more. Pleasantness and tension co-arise together and give rise to desire. On the other hand, if I like the macaroon and relax into the enjoyment, I may feel pleasure and satisfaction without wanting more. Desire depends on both the memory of pleasure and tension: they must co-arise:

**memory of pleasant feeling + tension → desire**

Or conversely:

**memory of unpleasant feeling + tension → aversion**

The tension can come from anywhere. If my life feels relaxed, my eating is motivated by the pleasant memory of food and the tension of hunger. If my life is stressed because of work, family, politics, or anything else, I may not need the tension of hunger to want to eat. I'll have plenty of free-floating tension already, which when it co-arises with the thought of pleasant food, is enough to make me want to eat (or overeat).

To reduce desire, we can't just shove the desire aside — that's aversion and it creates more tension. Also, we can't get rid of the pleasant memory any more than we can not think of a pink dragon flying upside down once the suggestion is made. However, we can relax the tension if we know what to look for and are willing to soften.

# Flowing Upstream

Another aspect of the paradox of paṭiccasamuppāda is how its flow can reverse. Usually the links/events flow "downstream" from subtle to coarse phenomena: from a stream to a river as it were. But sometimes the flow reverses. For example, how we see a person can affect how we feel about them, and how we feel about them can affect how we see them. Feeling warm and cozy can elicit thoughts in me about my cat, Lila. And thinking about Lila can elicit warm and cozy feelings. William James, the philosopher and psychologist, once asked, "Does a man run because he's scared of a bear or is he scared because he's running?"

I don't have a good analogy to explain why the flow can sometimes reverse, but it's easy to see. This may be why paṭiccasamuppāda is sometimes described as dependent origination and sometimes as dependent co-arising: the nidāna are definitely linked tightly together, and the influence can extend in both directions.

Perhaps part of the reason is because the brain is a multiprocessor. It has a vast number of circuits that can fire in parallel as well as in sequence. When awareness is soft and broad, we can get a glimpse of many things going on at once.

# Freedom

No matter how we translate the term, the key to unraveling paṭiccasamuppāda is to recognize that we are dealing with powerful forces in which tension is the key. The various nidāna are complex. They are the streambeds, river channels, lake basins, and ocean floors that give shape to paṭiccasamuppāda as described in maps and charts in chapter 9. But the most important factor is simple taṇhā. It is the water and energy that flows through those shapes and forms. If we carefully notice it and relax, then the water evaporates, paṭiccasamuppāda becomes empty, and we are free from flowing inevitably into suffering.

# Luminosity

When we look at the landscape around us, there is often a sense of self and other: an observer (me) watching other creatures and things out there. When we first look at our inner landscape, we start with a similar sense of an observer, me, watching things going on inside: a self that is noticed and an awareness that notices.

As our practice relaxes and opens more and more, self and other — the observer and the observed — start to merge into a luminous, nondual awareness. This kind of awareness can't be seen from the outside, though it can be known from the inside. Gradually, even outside and inside seem like arbitrary conventions.

This section explores this luminous knowing.

# 11

# Night Vision: Modes of Knowing

*When she was a young woman, my Great Auntie May hunted bear and fished in southern Ontario, Canada. She enjoyed the countryside so much, she bought a dozen acres along a beautiful lake and built a summer cottage.*

*Auntie May got married for the first time when she was 86 — she never had children of her own. However, she was close to her four nieces, one of whom was my mother. Over the years she gave parcels of her land to her nieces and their families so they could build their own cottages. The collective family encampment grew to include three cottages, a log cabin, a boathouse, and a geodesic dome.*

*When I was growing up, I enjoyed vacationing on that lake along with my cousins, aunts, and uncles. In the evenings, we'd gather in one of the cottages to play cards, work on puzzles, tell stories, and hang out.*

*When it was time to go back to our abodes, there were plenty of flashlights to light the paths through the dark. But I always refused a flashlight. I preferred others go ahead while I quietly gazed at the stars or the lake and listened to the night critters.*

*When my eyes had adjusted to the dark, I'd feel my way home. I loved being enfolded by the night. I loved feeling with my mind and sensing with my body. I never felt the darkness was a threat I had to protect myself from. I didn't try to figure out what those blurry images were as much as I just enjoyed the mystery. I didn't try to grab hold of or define what I really saw; I let the twilight reveal as much or as little as it liked. I grew to trust my instincts to guide me home. This way of seeing was fun in its own quiet way.*

*Everyone said I had good night vision. But I never believed my eyes were better than anyone else's. It wasn't a matter of visual acuity or of knowing exactly what I sensed. It was a matter of learning to trust internal sensing.*

## Anattā

In this final section of the book, I'd like to explore luminous, nondual awareness. This mode of knowing could be called "spiritual night vision." As a child, my night vision had two aspects: one was blurry visual images transmitted from my retina, and the other was all my other senses — hearing, feeling, intuiting, and more. When most of my family members were in the dark, they used flashlights to flood the woods with photons. In so doing, they relied solely on physical vision. But I enjoyed feeling my way through the dark. So I avoided bright flashlights, paid careful attention to those fuzzy images, and engaged my other senses. I don't think my intuitive sensing was initially better than anyone else's, but I enjoyed using it. With trial and error and lots of practice, it became better and better. My night vision got stronger, not because of seeing per se but because my seeing was aided by other ways of knowing.

So "spiritual night vision" means knowing with more than thoughts, words, and images. In the Buddhist text, it's associated with the Pāli word *anattā*. *Anattā* is usually translated as "no self," "non-self," or "no higher self." *Anattā* is one of the Buddha's central and most important teachings. And it may be the most confounding. At first glance, non-self is nonsense: "Of course I have a self. It's right here. It's obvious."

To understand anattā, it's tempting to define the term and explore what it meant to those people who first heard him use it. However, what's most important is not the term itself but cultivating spiritual night vision. Defining the term is like stepping into the dark woods and turning on a bright light: it temporarily eliminates the darkness rather than helps us navigate through it. And I think the

Buddha's first interest was cultivating the ability to navigate on our own without artificial light.

To say this differently, the Buddha's teachings about *anattā* are less about a thing to be understood and more about a way of understanding. It's less about seeing particular trees in the woods and more about cultivating intuitive night vision. It's less about what we know and more about modalities of knowing.

Let me explain what I mean by this.

# Modes of Knowing

There are different modes of knowing. Two of the most obvious are objective knowing and subjective knowing. They are as different as day and night, bright light and twilight, thoughts and feelings, blueprints and impressionist paintings. A third mode is often called "nondual" or "luminous." It is subtler than subjective awareness. At first it feels like groping in the dark.

Before we can fully appreciate anattā, we need some familiarity with nondual awareness. To appreciate nondual awareness, it helps to be familiar with objective and subjective awareness. So I'd like to explore all three of these modalities staring with objectivity and subjectivity. We'll look at nonduality in the next chapter.

### Objective Mode

When the Buddha spoke about anattā, he wasn't speaking objectively. Objective reality is made up of things known through the physical senses — things that can be seen, heard, touched, tasted, or smelled. Objectively we can know that the car has a flat tire, there is no milk in the refrigerator, the moon circles the earth, I'm six feet tall, and so forth. The objective realm is studied by physics, biology, astronomy, and other sciences where things can be counted, weighed, and measured. In the objective realm, everything has what the philosopher Alfred North Whitehead called "simple location" — we can find it in physical, three-dimensional space.

## Subjective Mode

Subjective reality is made up of things we can only know internally through the mind-heart. Meaning, spirituality, aesthetics, moral sensibilities, feelings, and value can't be physically seen, heard, touched, tasted, or smelled. They don't have simple locations. We can't find meaning in a box in the cupboard. We can feel love, anger, despair, joy, and gratitude. But they can't be stored on a shelf, counted on a spreadsheet, or pointed to in the external world.

While the objective and subjective worlds are very different, there can be correlations between them. For example, the brain is in the physical realm — it has simple location. The mind is in the inner realm — it doesn't have simple location. Certain brain activity corresponds to the memory of a romantic evening. But a brain wave is vastly different from a memory.

Nobody knows the mechanism by which a neural pattern and an image arise together. We don't even know causation: whether neural activity causes the memory or the memory causes the neural activity. We can just demonstrate correlations.

## Mode Preference

All cultures and all people experience both the objective and the subjective. Most understand that these two modes aren't the same. If we asked some pious, tenth-century European monks, "Objectively, did Moses actually part the Red Sea?" or "Did Jesus really walk on the water?" they probably would have answered, "Are you a dunderhead? Your questions make no sense." In medieval Europe, many understood that Biblical language and stories were not about the objective, literal, external world. They were about subjective inner meaning and spirituality that can only be known internally.

Though all of us can experience both the objective and subjective realms, different cultures place more emphasis on one than the other. Under the influence of the medieval church, the interior world was primary. If Biblical text conflicted with mundane observations, the Bible was considered more authoritative, even if it had to be taken on blind faith.

## Rise of Science

In the 15th and 16th centuries, the primacy of the interior world began to shift. People started to study the mundane world on its own terms rather than through church doctrine. To better see the objective world, Galileo invented the telescope. Looking through it, he saw moons circulating around Jupiter just like our moon circulates around the earth. He saw light and shadows shifting as if Jupiter was a giant ball circling the sun. He speculated that maybe the earth wasn't the center of the universe. Maybe the sun was the center and the earth and Jupiter moved around the sun.

The inquisitor said to Galileo, "The Bible says nothing about moons around Jupiter. Therefore, there are no moons around Jupiter and the earth does not move around the sun. And we are so confident that we don't even have to look through your devilish instrument. You must recant or face the consequences."

Galileo preferred not to face the consequences. He officially accepted church doctrine. But legend has it that, after recanting, he muttered under his breath, "Tamensi movetur!" which is Latin for "And yet she [the earth] moves."

The growing willingness of Galileo and others to look at the world objectively began to move science out from under the thumb of church orthodoxy. As it did, scientific inquiry flourished. Since then science has arguably done more to relieve human suffering than any other endeavor: life expectancy has more than doubled, scientific medicine has cured diseases, infant mortality has decreased, food production has increased, labor saving machines have been invented, new technologies have emerged, and on and on.

Science became so successful, that subjective and nondual modes of thinking began to seem quaint and passé. People forgot the difference between religious language and scientific inquiry. They began to read the Bible with the same mindset used to read a science report. Ironically, this gave rise to a new form of religious fundamentalism that treated the Bible as literal objective truth rather than internal subjective inquiry.

To be sure, various flavors of literalism can be found in early Christianity and as far back into human history as we can see. For example, a common form of literalism was ancestor worship, in which ancient religious authorities were considered sacrosanct. The words they passed down through ancient texts or oral transmission were treated as the final arbiters of truth. If I experienced something that conflicted with them, this was proof that life today had degenerated from a golden age of long ago.

What's new since the rise of science is not literalism per se but the use of pseudoscientific arguments to support ancient pronouncements. The Inquisitors made no attempt to counter Galileo's discoveries with rational scientific arguments. They just pointed to the Bible and said, "See, you're wrong." However, since the Western Enlightenment we've seen fundamentalists use pseudoscientific arguments to support religious literalism. For example, the 17th century chronographer James Ussher used the Bible to calculate that creation occurred on a Saturday evening, October 22, around 6 p.m. in 4004 BC.

## Loss of Meaning

As helpful as scientific objectivity has been, it has limitations when it dominates our thinking so much that we lose the ability to explore subjective questions about meaning, values, and ethics.

For example, we could ask, "Which is better: love or hate?" Most people say, "Love." But we can't validate this scientifically. Science can tell us the biological correlates of love and hate. It can survey people's feelings and tell us what they prefer. But it can't tell us which is better, because value is internal and subjective. Empirical science can't touch that realm.

Here's a more complex question: which is more important, generosity or accumulation? Generosity is an inner quality. Accumulation is external. Trying to use external accumulation to measure internal generosity can be confusing. If we save a lot of money, is it because internally we're stingy and self-centered? Or is it because we're generous and want to pay for our kid's college and pass on an inheritance when we die?

The material and subjective realms bump into each other. We need ways to talk about the inner life of value and meaning as well as the external requirements of food, clothing, shelter, and financial stability.

Today many people think the outer, objective world is "real" and the inner, subjective world is "unreal." They are both real. However, they appear differently, behave differently, are sensed differently, and use different kinds of language.

I first understood the different uses of language for these two modes from the writings of Carlos Castaneda. He was an anthropologist who trained with a shaman in the lineage of the ancient Toltecs. Castaneda wrote a series of books, starting with *The Teachings of Don Juan* in 1968.[31]

At one point Castaneda had an intense vision of flying while under the influence of peyote. Later he asked Don Juan if he had actually flown.

Don Juan said, "Of course. It's what you experienced."

Castaneda says, "No. I mean did I fly the way a bird flies?"

Don Juan looked at him like he was an idiot. "No," he said. "A bird flies the way a bird flies. You flew the way a human flies."

Castaneda continued to try to get Don Juan to validate his subjective experience with an objective external reference. Don Juan wouldn't be drawn in. Like some medieval monks, he knew the question was nonsense: the inner and outer worlds aren't the same. [32]

Don Juan's teachings went even further into what could be called nondual knowing — a luminous awareness most often experienced as "oneness," "flow," or "harmony."

---

[31] Carlos Castaneda, *The Teachings of Don Juan: A Yaqui Way of Knowledge* (New York: Ballantine Books, 1968).

[32] Some Buddhist texts refer to monks levitating. Did they really fly? Don Juan might say it's a wrongheaded question.

# Meditation and Modes of Knowing

Meditation is not about the objective world. The first thing we do when we meditate is remove ourselves from the external senses as much as is practical: we sit quietly in a physically comfortable place away from external distractions, and we close our eyes. We are seeking happiness, peace, contentment, awareness, insight, wisdom, and other inner qualities. None of these have simple location. The *jhānas*, compassion, *samādhi*, joy, equanimity, spaciousness, the realm of nothingness, *nirodha*, and so forth can only be known internally.

However we translate *anattā* — non-self, no unchanging self, no enduring soul essence — is not about the external world or the physical senses. The Buddha goes to great lengths to say that anattā is not an objective experience. In the "Chachakka Sutta: Six Sets of Six" (*Majjhima Nikāya* 148), he goes methodically through all the physical senses, saying that self is not in an external sensory object (such as light or sound), it's not in a sensory organ (such as the eye or ear), and it's not in a sensory experience (such as seeing or hearing).

He goes on to say that self is not in the subjective world either. It's not in subjective mental objects such as thoughts or images, in subjective states such as feeling tone or desire, or in the subjective awareness of those feelings, desires, and urges.

So what's left?

## No Thingness

To describe what's left, let's walk through the highest *jhānas,* or stages of meditation. When we get into the Buddha's seventh *jhāna* or "the Realm of Nothingness," nothing registers from the objective world. A better label might be "no thingness" because we no longer attend to external things. We may still notice subjective phenomena: feelings, moods, qualities of mind and heart, inner lights, and so forth. But there are no more thoughts about the weather, what's for lunch, whether we have enough cat food, or anything else about the mundane world.

The inner quiet that is required to get into this space may allow old forgotten feelings, memories, and impressions from the past to surface. If they come into awareness and are not immediately released, we can be drawn out of the *jhāna* and into old stories.

I spent several years parked in the *seventh* jhāna while meditating. New and old tensions kept surfacing. I learned to use the Six Rs to recognize and release old psychological material. It was a kind of purification. But I couldn't go further.

I told my teacher, Bhante Vimalaraṁsi, "*I* can't get into the eighth jhāna," with an emphasis on "I." He laughed and said, "That's right. As long as a 'you' is there as an object, you won't go into the eighth." As long as I identified with any experience, liked or disliked anything, I remained beholden to the subjective realm of the seventh jhāna.

In time I relaxed and released enough to not grab hold of each memory and insight. They no longer stuck with me. This is the training ground of no thingness — learning to release the subjective world of feelings, memories, pain, yearnings, fears, and all the subjective stuff that I identified with so dearly.

### Fading of Perception

As I learned to release these old identities, perception of the subjective world began to fade as well. I finally went into the eighth jhāna. There was still perception and awareness, but not of the objective or subjective worlds. At this stage, yogis often can't figure out where they are. They may even wonder if they can be asleep and awake at the same time. Perception here doesn't feel like ordinary perception. But it doesn't feel like there's no perception either. Hence it's called "the realm of neither-perception-nor-non-perception." Awareness is faint in this realm. It can feel like groping in the woods in the night without a flashlight. And it's very peaceful.

This is what's left when the objective and subjective fade. It could be called "clear, luminous awareness." Very little is left but awareness itself. And that awareness is clear, kind, insightful, agendaless, relaxed, uplifted, luminous, intimate, and completely impersonal. It just is.

This is the space where anattā — selflessness — becomes obvious. There is just a flow of phenomena. No solid self. No solid objects of any kind. Not even subjective emotions. Just a flow of phenomena.

The meditation instructions are to let awareness rest in the clear luminosity. If anything at all arises, just let it relax immediately. I understood these instructions as "Do nothing. Six-R everything."

So, if you want to know what the Buddha meant by *anattā*, all you have to do is get into the eighth jhāna and it will reveal itself. The Buddha's path of jhānas leads right to this luminous, nondual mode of awareness.[33]

Perhaps you've experienced the seventh and eighth jhānas. Perhaps not. However, even without the upper jhānas or without familiarity with the label "nondual," I believe many people have some sense of this glowing awareness. It feels similar to night vision: groping in the dark woods while trusting the mind to sense things we can't see clearly.

# Nondual Language

In the next chapter, we'll explore other ways to directly experience the nondual mode of knowing. In the process, we'll gradually shift to a nondual use of language. It feels different than objective or subjective language. The topic of this chapter has been different modes of knowing — specifically objective, subjective, and nondual. However, the language used to describe these modalities has been objective. This is the most common modality today.

If we want to truly understand the Buddha's teachings, sooner or later we must shift both our mode of awareness and our use of language to luminous nondual. We'll do this in the next chapter.

---

[33] The jhānas are stages of meditation which the Buddha spoke about often. The highest jhānas move into nondual awareness. For a more detailed description of all the jhānas and how to work with them in meditation, see Doug Kraft, *Buddha's Map*.

# 12

# Nondual Experience

Our grandson, Henry, is a toddler. When it's time for him to go to bed, his mom and dad make the world as boring as possible. They quietly put away toys — often he helps. They turn down the lights. They speak in soft voices.

During a recent visit, his mom added another element to the ritual. She picked him up to light a candle as his dad turned off the lights. Carrying him to a second candle, she softly sang, "This little light of mine, I'm gonna let it shine...." The rest of us joined in. "This little light of mine, I'm gonna let it shine...."

Henry was totally charmed. He grew still as he savored the glow in the room. "Let it shine, let it shine, let it shine."

Our singing drifted into silence. Henry was just present, taking it all in. Then he lifted his hands slowly and touched his fingertips together several times. A baby's ability to mentally understand language matures faster than the verbal ability to articulate sounds. So he and his parents had learned some sign language. He was signing "more."

We sang more: "Everywhere I go, I'm gonna let it shine...."

When the verse faded, he seemed to glow like the candles. He brushed his fingers tips down the side of his head — the sign for "sleep."

"Goodnight, dada," his mom said for him. "Goodnight grandma. Goodnight grandpa." He looked at us with glistening eyes. We gently blew him kisses. He snuggled into his mom as she carried him to bed.

How can we describe his state of mind-heart? One label is "luminous, nondual awareness."

"Luminous, nondual awareness" may sound sophisticated, complex, esoteric, and something for advanced yogis. But it seemed that this was what Henry was experiencing. As I noted in the last chapter (p. 173), nondual awareness is simple, preverbal, clear, agendaless, nonjudging, relaxed, uplifted, and luminous in that it spreads out rather than focuses in. It's also patiently present with things as they are; and is whole rather than split into past and future, us and them, this and that. It is primal in that it undergirds all awareness though we are usually too busy to notice it. It is simple and innocent.

We might ask, "Where do we find luminous nondual awareness? How can it be cultivated?" The answers are, "It's right under our noses" and "It can't be cultivated because it's already here." Even a baby can know it. We all know nondual awareness, though we may forget we know.

A familiar Sufi story makes the point:

*A man saw his friend searching for something under a streetlight.*

*"What did you lose?" he asked.*

*"My key," the friend replied.*

*The man joined the search. But alas, they couldn't find the key.*

*"Where did you lose it?"*

*"Inside," his friend said as he fingered through a tuft of grass.*

*The man exclaimed, "Inside! Why are you looking out here?"*

*As his friend looked under a stone for the third time, he replied patiently, "The light's better out here."*

## Anattā

In the last chapter we began searching for *anattā*, one of the Buddha's most enigmatic teachings. In Pāli, the language of the suttas, *attā* means "self" and *an-* is a negation. So anattā is usually translated as "not self" or "non-self."

However, the "self" that *attā* refers to is not our ordinary, everyday self. It is a "higher self" or "eternal, unchanging soul essence" as described in the ancient Vedic texts.

So when the Buddha created the term *anattā*, his contemporaries would have understood it to mean "no permanent, timeless, higher self-essence" rather than "no self." Richard Gombrich translates *anattā* as "no unchanging self."[34] This definition of anattā is easier to grasp. But still, the notion slips away easily.

Another way to describe anattā is "everything is process." Unfortunately, the Pāli and Sanskrit languages have no clear word for process. Because it wasn't in the Buddha's lexicon, he used metaphors such as "arising and passing," "impermanence," and "no unchanging self" to point to what we would call "process."[35]

Part of the difficulty is not just the words themselves, but the way we use language today. The last chapter explored objective and subjective modes of knowing and languaging and introduced nonduality. Most of our language today is objective. It's like a bright streetlight illuminating the surface. However, anattā can only be found deep inside. It's like feeling our way through the woods at night or looking inside a dark room: meaning can be sensed but not grasped.

In this chapter, rather than talk about the various modes of knowing, we'll step into them. The nondual mode of knowing cannot be adequately explained from outside nonduality, no matter how bright the streetlights. If we want to cultivate night vision, at some point we must step into the dark and give it a try. I'll begin by describing anattā using the three modes of language: objective scientific, subtle internal feeling, and evocative nondual.

---

[34] Richard Gombrich, *What the Buddha Thought* (Sheffield, UK and Bristol, CT: Equinox, 2010), p. 9.
[35] Ibid. pp. 8–11.

Because anattā is one of the Buddha's central teachings, various teachers have tried to explain non-self objectively and subjectively. So I'll begin with objective and subjective descriptions. As you read these, I invite you to pay attention to how your mind feels rather than just to what you think of the subject matter.

# Objective Scientific Mode

First, let's look at anattā using objective, external, scientific language.

## Whirlpool

My favorite scientific analogy suggests that self is like a whirlpool. Along the American River where I live, the contours of the bank sometimes turn the water around and force it to flow back upstream for a short distance. When the upstream flow rubs against the downstream momentum of the main river, whirlpools spin off.

I find the phenomena fascinating, even mesmerizing. A whirlpool is a distinctive event, but nothing in it essentially distinguishes it from the river itself. Without the river, the whirlpool could not exist at all.

The center of the whirlpool is nothing — just air or a hole in the water. The center of the whirlpool is empty of whirlpool-ness. Water spins around the emptiness and gives it an undulating shape. The spinning water is no different from the water in the rest of the river. And when the whirlpool moves away from the conditions that caused it to arise — when it spins away from the confluence of the upstream and downstream flows — the energy dissipates, the spinning slows down, the hole fills in, and the whirlpool blends back into the river.

Nothing real is lost. The water is still there. The energy that spun around is still in the river even though it is not spinning in the same way. Even the air remains above the water. The pattern is gone, but all the elements of the pattern are still present.

We are like whirlpools in that everything in our bodies, our thoughts, and our energies comes from the larger river of life. We spin around ourselves in a temporary pattern whose essence is emptiness. When we die, our pattern may be lost — but that was just a temporary abstraction. Nothing that made us up is gone. It goes on in a different pattern. And even when our pattern is strong and apparent, its core is empty.

## Water

My second favorite objective description of self comes from the British philosopher Julian Baggini. In a TED talk[36], he projects a circle on the screen with the word "Water" in the middle and asks, "What is water?"

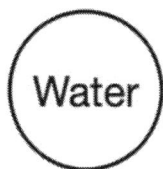

From our high school science, we know that water is made up of two hydrogen atoms and one oxygen atom: $H_2O$. So he adds these to the diagram. Then he asks, "What's the matter with this picture?"

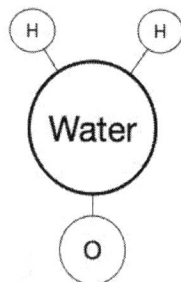

The problem is that the diagram implies that we can take away the hydrogen and oxygen and still have the water right there in the middle. But without those three atoms, there would be no water. In fact, if we take even one of them away, it becomes something very different from water.

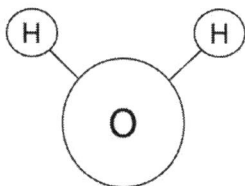

So he removes the circle containing the word "Water," leaving the more familiar diagram of a water molecule.

Finally, he superimposes on that molecule the label "Water." It's dim and floats over the molecule, indicating that it's an abstraction. There is no *waterness* in the water molecule apart from its three elements. "Water" is an umbrella term that refers to a specific configuration. It doesn't

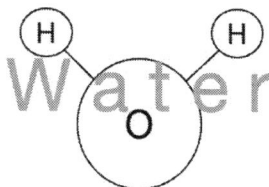

---

[36] See https://www.ted.com/talks/julian_baggini_is_there_a_real_you.

exist by itself. In reality, there are just the atoms arranged as a molecule.

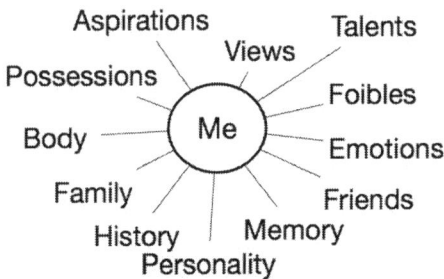

Aspirations    Talents
Views
Possessions
Foibles
Body    Me
Emotions
Family    Friends
History    Memory
Personality

We apply Baggigini's notion easily to just about everything in life except for ourselves. For example, we know a car is made up of many parts. Take all those parts away, and there is no car. But with self, we might imagine a circle with the word *Me* in the middle. Connected to it are attributes: body parts, emotions, intellect, memories, neuroses, hang-ups, talents, dreams, fears, and all the rest.

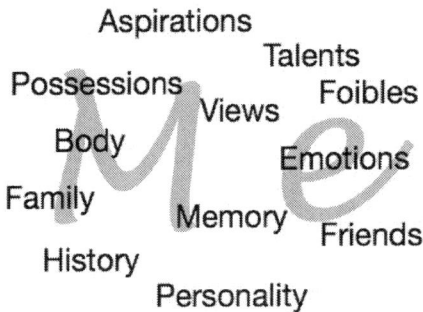

Aspirations
Talents
Possessions    Foibles
Views
Body    Emotions
Family    Memory    Friends
History
Personality

But of course, there is no me-in-a-circle inside us any more than there is water-in-a-circle inside an $H_2O$ molecule. If we take those parts away, there is no "me" left. "Me" is just an umbrella term — an abstraction — that points to a collection of qualities. There is no me-ness distinct from its parts.

After reading these objective explanations of anattā, pause and shift your attention from the content of the descriptions to the quality of your awareness. How does the mind feel when it's in the objective mode? We'll want to compare this to how the mind feels in other modes.

# Inner Subjective Anattā

Let's shift to the inner subjective mode. What is self like in the subjective realm?

*James Finley is an author who trained with Thomas Merton. His mother, whom I'll call "Sarah," grew up attending a Catholic academy. She was especially fond of one of her teachers, Sister Julia. They stayed in touch long after she graduated.[37]*

*Many years later, Sister Julia had dementia and was dying. Sarah went to visit her beloved teacher. It was the Christmas season. She bought a beautiful rosary and wrapped it up as a Christmas gift.*

*When Sarah went into Sister Julia's room, the nun was sitting up in bed. Sarah offered the gift to her, "Merry Christmas." Sister Julia said, "Thank you very much" and placed it on a bedside table.*

*The two women talked for a while. When the conversation drifted around to the Christmas season, Sister Julia looked at the gift package, picked it up, and said, "I have a Christmas present for you." Apparently, the nun completely forgot that Sarah had just given it to her.*

*Sarah accepted the gift. Not knowing quite what to do with it, she just held it in her hand.*

*Sister Julia said, "Well, aren't you going to open it?"*

*So Sarah opened it and pulled the rosary out of its box.*

*Sister Julia asked, "Do you like it?"*

*Sarah said, "It's lovely."*

*Sister Julia said, "I'm so pleased. I wanted you to be happy."*

*Years later Sarah still treasured that rosary as one of the most precious gifts she'd ever received.*

If we look at the story only through external references of objects with simple location, it is the confused nonsense of a demented woman. If we look at it through the subjective realm of feelings and values, it is deeply moving. It is imbued with kindness, generosity, innocence, love, and selflessness. This is what anattā means in subjective, inner experience.

The objective and subjective experiences of anattā are very different. Objective anattā is about physical objects, whirlpools,

---

[37] James Finley, *Meister Eckhart's Living Wisdom: Indestructible Joy and the Path of Letting Go* recorded by *Sounds True* on June 1, 2014, CD, https://www.soundstrue.com/store/meister-eckhart-s-living-wisdom-5959.html.

body parts, and so forth. Subjective anattā is inner experience no matter your psychological condition: emotions, feelings, connection, ease, and so forth.

But the feelings and emotions we associate with the subjective are not what the Buddha meant by "anattā."

# Nondual Luminous Anattā

Now let's try on a nondual, luminous way of talking about anattā. Here, language is not meant to tell us what something is. It is meant to touch an understanding we already have but may have forgotten. It doesn't try to define anything as much as resonate with a shadowy awareness that is waiting to be acknowledged. The language is poetic and evocative. With our culture's recent emphasis on external knowing, the art of nondual knowing is under-exercised.

One of the masters of this kind of language was Meister Eckhart, a Christian mystic who was born in 1260 in Germany when nondual Christianity was alive and well.

For example, he wrote:

*I am not God.*
*I am not other than God either.*
*Let that soak in for a moment.*

He was drawing on an ancient tradition called *via negativa,* or "way of negation." It posits logical contradictions to confound the objective mind. And at the same time it evokes a deeper, instinctive recognition that each negation has some truth to it: We are God. And we aren't God. And we are not other than God.

Let those soak in as well.

With modern fundamentalism and all the conflicting ways we use religious terms, words like "God" may be too charged to leave room for the sensing of subtle direct experience.

So here is a contemplation in the style of *via negativa* and Meister Eckhart that's been adapted for Buddhists. Relax and see what this language evokes in you:

*I am not you,*
    *Neither am I other than you.*
*I am not the community of creatures,*
    *Neither am I other than all creatures.*

*I am not the earth,*
    *Neither am I other than the earth.*
*I am not space,*
    *Neither am I other than space.*
*I am not enlightened,*
    *Neither am I other than enlightened.*
*I am not a Buddha,*
    *Neither am I other than Buddha.*

One of the ways we create a sense of self is to identify consciously or unconsciously with various phenomena. Many of us identify with our thoughts: "They are my thoughts. They are me." As Descartes put it, *"Cognito, ergo sum."* ("I think, therefore I am.") If we can loosen that identification, we may loosen the sense of a self. So here is a contemplation on thought:

*Thinking happens by itself.*
    *Thinking arises.*
    *Thinking vanishes.*
*I am not thought,*
    *Neither am I other than thought.*
*I am not the witness of thinking,*
    *Neither am I other than the witness.*
*I am not what's aware of the witness,*
    *Neither am I other than awareness.*
*Awareness arises.*
*Awareness vanishes.*

The Buddha did not use *via negativa* in the traditional Christian style. But he used negation a lot — talking about what things are not. Some of his language can sound obscure unless we drop into the nondual modality.

Don't get entangled in the literal, objective meaning of the following words of the Buddha from *Udāna* 1.10. Using your spiritual night vision, relax and see what faint impressions they evoke:

*Where water, earth, fire, and wind have no footing:*
*There the stars don't shine, the sun isn't visible.*
*There the moon doesn't appear.*
*There darkness is **not** found.*
*And when a sage through wisdom*
    *has known this for himself,*
*then from form and formless,*
    *from bliss and pain,*
        *he is freed....*

Water, earth, fire, and wind are four of the "five great elements" of the Vedic tradition, which the Buddha knew well. They are not to be confused with the modern, scientific elements of the periodic table. In ancient times the water element referred to fluidity and cohesion. The earth referred to solidity. Fire referred to heat. Wind referred to motion. The fifth element was space. So the first line is alluding to space without anything tangible in it — the elements "have no footing."

To say this differently, space contains everything we can know through the senses. Imagine space with nothing in it. There is not even a source of light — "the stars don't shine, the sun isn't visible. There the moon doesn't appear." Yet imagine this space being self-illuminated: "There darkness is not found." This could be called "bright, clear mind" or "luminous mind" that is empty of all things and yet is knowable. It's illuminated only by itself.

The Buddha is not asking us to employ conventional thinking or logic. When the Zen master Hakuin Ekaku asked "You know the sound of two hands clapping; tell me, what is the sound of one hand?" he was not asking for a scientific demonstration. The language was meant to evoke something we cannot count, weigh, or measure. But we can sense it with spiritual night vision.

Rather than analyze the text logically, we're invited to let the images seep in and see what they evoke. The Buddha says, when we can do this fully, we are free. We awaken.

The *Udāna* 8.1 presents a similar poem that invites us to go beyond the objective and subjective, and beyond the three highest *jhānas* — infinite space, infinite consciousness, and neither-perception-nor-non-perception. Our awareness goes beyond all worldly conventions. Notice that the Buddha doesn't say what this is, only what it is not: *via negativa*. It is for us to feel our way through that twilight to the end of suffering and to full awakening:

> *There is that mode where there is neither earth, nor water, nor fire, nor wind;*
> *neither the infinitude of space,*
> *nor the infinitude of consciousness,*
> *nor nothingness, neither perception nor non-perception;*
> *neither this world, nor the next world, nor sun, nor moon.*
> *And there is neither coming, nor going, nor staying;*
> *neither passing away nor arising,*
> *neither coming to be nor change,*
> *without perception.*
> *This, just this, is the end of suffering.*

Again, just relax tensions and let these images and what they may be pointing to soak in.

Perhaps the most famous of the Buddha's nondual texts is the *Diamond Sutra* of Mahayana Buddhism. Here the word "empty" means that something is empty of itself. For example, a flower is possible because of seeds, soil, rain, sun, and all of nature. Within the flower, there is no flower essence that is separate from the rest of life. The flower is made entirely of non-flower elements. So it exists conventionally, but it has no absolute existence as a separate essence. It is just a temporary configuration that arises out of the web of nature. Relax, settle in, and see what the words evoke:

> *All things are empty:*
> *Nothing is born, nothing dies,*
> *nothing is pure, nothing is stained,*
> *nothing increases and nothing decreases.*
>
> *There is no ignorance,*
> *and no end to ignorance.*
> *There is no old age and death,*
> *and no end to old age and death.*
> *There is no suffering, no cause of suffering,*
> *no end to suffering, no path to follow.*
> *There is no attainment of wisdom,*
> *and no wisdom to attain.*

Finally, one of the greatest of the Eastern nondual sages was Lao Tzu. He lived and died roughly a century before the Buddha. We have very few of his actual words compared to the volumes of texts attributed to the Buddha. But his language was clearly nondual. Here is an example:

> *Desires wither the heart.*
> *The sage observes the world*
> *but trusts his inner vision.*
> *He allows things to come and go.*
> *His heart is open as the sky.*
>
> *True mastery can be gained*
> *by letting things go their own way.*
> *It can't be gained by interfering.*
>
> *All things are born of being.*
> *Being is born of nonbeing.*[38]

---

[38] Lao Tzu, *Tao Te Ching*, trans. Stephen Mitchel (London: France Lincoln, Lid, 1988), verse 12.

# 13

# Practicing Wisdom

Any exploration of anattā and oneness is incomplete without Shantideva. He was an eighth-century Indian prince and seeker who is considered second only to the Buddha in shaping and articulating Buddhist understanding. He wrote in a dialectical style that uses logic in a strict and formal manner. He wrote, in effect, "If I have a permanent, unchanging self-essence, then I cannot grow or change. If I can grow or change, then I have no unchanging essence."

Intuitively we may feel that we have an unchanging essence, soul, or higher self. And intuitively we may feel that we can learn and grow. Shantideva points out that we can't have it both ways. If we can change, we aren't permanent. If we are permanent, we can't change.

When I first read his argument, I was tempted to rebut him by asserting that I can grow and learn on the surface as I discover my real unchanging self underneath. But unless I'm fully enlightened, how do I know that I have a true, core self? It's just a blind assertion that I don't really know.

So, to be fully honest with myself, I have to say, "I don't really know if there is a true self that doesn't change or grow but might be discoverable." This is all the Buddha is asking of us: keep an open mind about the question of self-essence. Shantideva and the Buddha go on to say that they don't see anything permanent.

If we have no core permanency, this has implications for our meditation practice and for daily life.

Shantideva composed a long poem called *The Bodhisattva's Way* which elaborates on anattā and its implications. A bodhisattva is a person who vows to help liberate all beings from suffering. The last chapter of the poem is called "Wisdom." It is the heart of his commentary.

The Dalai Lama has written extensively about Shantideva, including an entire book on that last chapter. The title of the Dalai Lama's book is *Practicing Wisdom*. The title isn't "What Is Wisdom," "Being Wise," or even "Attaining Wisdom." It is "Practicing Wisdom." The Buddha, Shantideva, and the Dalai Lama use anattā as a verb — something we do — rather than as a noun — something we are, hold, or aspire to. *Anattā* is a practice to be engaged, not a point of view to be articulated or grasped. Shantideva's title, *The Bodhisattva's Way*, suggests *anattā* is a way of traveling rather than a destination.

By the way, one popular understanding of the bodhisattva vow is misguided. That view says that by taking this vow, I am promising to liberate all beings before I allow myself to enter *nibbāna* or become liberated. It's like promising to be a spiritual Atlas lifting the entire world — or at least all beings — onto my shoulders and carrying them across the finish line before I cross that line myself.

The problem with that interpretation is too much selfing. I promise to be a martyr, a savior, a crusader rabbit who will take care of everyone else before taking care of me. It reinforces the false narrative of "Me...me...me..."

To be sure, this narrative has been bred into us by evolutionary selection. As mentioned earlier (p. 132), ancestors who cherished a separate self above all others were more likely to pass on their DNA than those who felt we are all One so everything's cool.

The true bodhisattva vow assumes that knowledge of Oneness remains deep inside us obscured by a felt imperative to protect our imagined separateness and to reproduce. Because it's already in us, we don't have to impose a belief in Oneness upon ourselves. If we engage and practice in ways that resonate with Oneness, the truth of it will awaken from its slumber.

The thirteenth century Zen monk, Dōgen, wrote:

*To study the way is to study the self.*
*To study the self is to lose the self.*
*To lose the self is to be enlightened by all things.*
*To be enlightened by all things is to remove the barrier between self and other.* [39]

So let's play along. What if we were deeply confident that, despite superficial separateness, there is no essential difference between self and other, you and me, us and all beings? What if we all are just part of the flow of energy and matter called "life"? How might this influence our practice and our way of being in the world? Here are some ways this might shape our practice:

- Resist nothing, hold nothing
- No battles, no wars
- No grabbing, no destination
- Let things come and go on their own
- Impersonal language
- Less personal will, more flow
- No self, no hindrance

Even if we aren't deeply confident in the depth and power of nondual wisdom, practicing in ways that resonate with nondual awareness may awaken it within us. So let's look at some of the ways to practice wisdom that awaken nondual awareness.

# Resist Nothing, Hold Nothing

If there is no self-essence, then there is nothing to be protected from the impersonal flow of phenomena. And when the phenomena are lovely, there's no self to hold on to the flow.

---

[39] This verse is also quoted at the end of chapter 2.

When people first start meditating, they often do the opposite. They resist thoughts, images, memories, hindrances, distractions, irritations, and other things that impinge on what they want. At the same time they try to hold onto ease, contentment, and other lovely phenomena. Resisting and holding create and strengthen a sense of self. When we don't resist or hold, the mirage of selfhood dissolves back into the flow of life.

So as we learn to meditate, when an unpleasant phenomenon seems to press in on us, we just recognize what's happening. Awareness is good and part of aliveness. We see the phenomena without trying to control it. We let it be. We relax any tension. We smile to resonate with uplifted qualities. Rather than holding on to lovely states, we return to sending them out into the flow of life. If some deeper insight into life starts to emerge like a shadow in the twilight, we don't try to grab hold of it or push it away. We just let it be what it is. As with night vision, we let the insight come to us rather than try to grab hold of it.

In other words, we Six-R without resistance and without holding.

That is one way to practice wisdom.

## No Battles, No Wars

Another way to say this is, "Don't struggle." As Adyashanti puts it: "If we oppose the mind, we will be at war forever."[40]

If there is no self-essence separate from everything else in life, then there can be no "true self" that is separate from an "everyday self." There is no inner witness separate from what's being witnessed. No subject or object.

When we close our eyes, there are just experiences. What we call "mind" is just a field of awareness. It isn't a separate thing. Awareness happens without a self doing awareness. Awareness is a

---

[40] Also quoted on p. 1.

mystery that doesn't stand apart from what's seen. There is awareness. There is no self-essence.

If this doesn't make sense, it's okay. Don't worry about it. Just don't battle with the mind and it will gradually become clear as your night vision adjusts.

This is another way to practice wisdom.

## No Grabbing, No Destination

If there is no separate self, there is no one to grab and no one to be grabbed; there is nothing to fix and no one to be fixed. There is just experiencing of grabbing that arises without a separate self to grab or be grabbed.

One of the common metaphors for spiritual development is a seeker on a journey. But if there is no seeker, then there is no one to go on a journey. If there's no self, there is nowhere for it to go.

This doesn't mean that life feels cold and heartless. Quite the opposite. As Carlos Castaneda put it in *The Teachings of Don Juan*:

> *Does this path have a heart? If it does, the path is good; if it doesn't it is of no use. Both paths lead nowhere; but one has a heart, the other doesn't. One makes for a joyful journey; as long as you follow it, you are one with it. The other will make you curse your life. One makes you strong; the other weakens you.*

As philosophical propositions, to say there is no place to go and no one to get there may clash with what we've been taught all our lives. But if we relax the sense of grabbing something or getting somewhere in favor of being present with what is, the sense of a separate self begins to flow into and harmonize with life itself.

## Let Things Come and Go on Their Own

It's very easy to fall into the trap of trying to get something in meditation — to find special lovely experiences. In beginning meditation we can get away with it to a degree. But as the practice deepens, the effort to draw forth special experiences blots out refined awareness. It is more helpful to let experiences find us rather

than us look for them. It is more skillful to surrender into the
moment than to look for the moment we want.

# Impersonal Language

We don't experience self directly. We never have. We experience
a sensation, a thought, a feeling tone. From this simple experience
we extrapolate "outward" to try to figure out what gave rise to the
sensation or thought. And we extrapolate "inward" to image what
or who had that experience. But these are extrapolations, not direct
experiences. We extrapolate so effortlessly and so constantly that we
don't even notice we are extrapolating. But the further we go in
trying to deduce the object and subject of the experience, the further
we get from actual experience. All we ever know directly is
experience itself. Who or what has the experience is just a guess.

Yet the very structure of language demands a subject doing
something: for example, "I am meditating." "I had a lovely feeling."
To leave out the subject — the "I" — sounds awkward. But it's closer
to our raw experience. So describing experience impersonally may
help the ubiquitous self relax or dissolve. We might say, "Happiness
arose," "The mind was busy thinking," or "There was fear." If we
develop the habit of talking about our experience using impersonal
language, it helps the mind notice that there is just experience
without an experiencer — thoughts without a thinker, feelings
without a feeler.

Anattā is not the point of nonduality. It is just one of the
byproducts. It's the nondual modality itself that most interested the
Buddha. Impersonal language can help evoke this way of sensing.

# Less Personal Will, More Flow

Another way to evoke impersonal language is to relax our
apparent drive and focus more on the on-going flow of experience.
As we attune less to our personal will and more to the continuous
flow of experience, the sense of self may recede into a sense of
oneness, flow, or spaciousness.

# No Self, No Hindrance

Learning how to relate to hindrances is a very important — perhaps the most important — aspect of meditation training. However, as Mr. Miyagi said in the movie *The Karate Kid*, "The best way to receive a punch is not to be there." The best way to deal with a hindrance is to not be there.

So when a hindrance arises, rather than shifting our attention to how to deal with the hindrance, we can shift attention to the sense of self that thinks it's experiencing a hindrance.

As described in the exercise on page 28, we can look inside for the sense of self. Once we notice where it resides, we can look at what that sense of self actually feels like and let the tension in it soften. As the tension subsides, sense of self lightens or diminishes, and the hindrance has nothing to push or pull. It ceases to be a problem: it's just another phenomenon.

It's like tug of war where one side lets go of the rope. Without a subject, the hindrance has nothing to struggle with. It fades into the impersonal flow of energy — not a problem. Eventually it may evaporate completely.

# *Oceans and Thimbles*

There are lots of other ways to practice wisdom — to treat wisdom as a way to engage life rather than a magic object to be found or possessed. Our intuition may offer other ways to practice wisdom.

I'll close with one more image. It's said that we can't put the ocean in a thimble but that we can put a thimble in the ocean.

We are the thimble.

We can't put luminous, nondual awareness into our tiny self. But we can immerse that little self in luminosity. It feels like surrender — surrendering out of our hyper-individualism into the ocean of life itself. As the small mind surrenders, there can be a touch of sadness or poignancy. We can let that dissolve into the ocean as well:

> *A lone bird floats in the dusk light. There is a softness, a fullness; a sense of completeness, of closure. A taste of grief, perhaps, at the waning of the day's life. To open to this moment is to be touched by the movement of life itself — even as it fades.*

> *Coming home is returning out of individuality and all its frenetic energy. The loss of self that comes with peace can be sad. The hand that held on so strongly for so long aches as it relaxes its grip. The merge may seem scary. We would avoid it if we could. But at some point it seems that this is all there is to do. So, we gradually let go.*

> *Love begins to penetrate the aching. The boundlessness of the sea has been waiting patiently for so long. The hurt softens, dissolves. How could I have stayed away from this for so long? Yes. This is Home.*

# Appendices

# Glossary

Different kinds of glossary entries are denoted by their formatting:

- Pāli terms are in *lowercase italics*.
- Sutta Titles are in *Title Case Italics*.
- Names of people and places are in Title Case Roman. People who were not a contemporary of the Buddha have an asterisk (*) after their name.
- English words that have a special meaning in Buddhism are displayed in lowercase roman.
- <u>Underlined</u> words have their own glossary entry that can be looked up for more information.

A more extended glossary can be found on the web at https://www.dougkraft.com/?p=Glossary.

*acinteyya*
>Imponderable; incomprehensible; questions or topics that cannot be answered and are vexing or crazy-making to try to solve. There are four topics the Buddha considered to be *acinteyya*: What are the powers of an enlightened being? What can meditation ultimately achieve? What karma caused a specific event to occur? Where did the universe come from?

Adyashanti*
>An American born spiritual teacher living in northern California whose teachings resonate with early Zen masters and Advaita Vedānta. See http://www.adyashanti.org.

Ānanda
>The Buddha's cousin and disciple and his primary attendant for the last half of his life. He was known for being able to hear a talk once and remember every word perfectly.

*Anguttara Nikāya*
　The fourth of the five nikāyas in the <u>*Sutta Pitaka*</u> is also known
　as the "Numerical Discourses" because it's organized
　according to the number of dhamma items referenced in each
　of its several thousand discourses.

*anattā (Sanskrit: atman)*
　No unchanging self. Not taking things personally. Selflessness.
　<u>*Attā*</u> means "self," and *an-* is a negation. So anattā is often
　translated as "no self." But since the Buddha's contemporaries
　often believed in a higher, eternal, unchanging, true self, those
　listening to the Buddha would have understood the word to
　mean no eternal, unchanging self-essence. (See *attā*)

Anuruddha
　One of the ten principal disciples and a cousin of the Buddha.

*asātanti*
　Unpleasing. (See *sātam*)

*attā (Sanskrit: atman)*
　Self or soul. The Buddha used the negation, <u>*anattā,*</u> to say that
　we have no unchanging eternal self.

*Atthaka Vagga*
　A small set of sixteen suttas that are believed to be among the
　earliest existing Buddhist literature. It is preserved as the
　fourth book of the <u>*Sutta Nipata*</u>.

*ariyo aṭṭhaṅgiko maggo*
　Eightfold path; noble eightfold path. This is the fourth of the
　Four Ennobling Truths. It consists of eight items that can be
　used to fine tune meditation practice.

*avijjā (Sanskrit: avidyā)*
　Unawareness, ignorance, <u>delusion</u> about the nature of the
　mind. *Avijjā* is commonly translated as "ignorance," though it
　has fewer pejorative connotations than in English. As in
　English, the root is "ignore" and indicates a tendency to
　overlook the true nature of things. *Avijjā* is the beginning of the
　downstream flow of <u>dependent origination</u> (<u>*paticcasamuppāda*</u>).
　Without it there would be no suffering.

awakening factors *(bojjhanga)*
Seven factors of the mind-heart that are conducive to awakening, particularly when they are brought into balance together. There are three energizing factors: investigation (dhamma vicaya), energy (viriya), and joy (piti). There are three calming factors: calm/tranquility (passaddhi), collectedness (samadhi) and equanimity (upekkha). There is one so-called neutral factor, mindfulness (sati) that can both energize or calm depending on what's needed.

*āyatana*
Sense medium. The inner sense media are the sense organs: eyes, ears, nose, tongue, body, and mind. The outer sense media are their respective objects (sights, sounds, etc.).

*bhante*
Title used to address a monk or nun. It literally means "Venerable Sir" and may be used for a monk or a nun.

Bhante Vimalaraṁsi*
An American Buddhist monk who is currently Abbot of the Dhamma Sukha Meditation Center in Annapolis, Missouri. He ordained in northern Thailand in 1986. From 1991 to 2000, he studied and practiced the _suttas_ intensely. He trained with many Asian teachers and may be best known for the Six R practice and for teaching the awareness _jhānas_.

*bhāva*
Habitual tendency or habitual emotional tendency. It is the tenth movement in the flow of <u>dependent origination</u> (_paticcasamuppāda_). It is often translated as "becoming" or "existence," but these meanings are confusing. In meditation, *bhava* is experienced as the arising of familiar or habitual patterns of thought and emotion.

*bhāvanā*
Mental development; meditation. The word originally was an agricultural term meaning "cultivation."

*bhikkhu*
An ordained male monastic in Buddhism.

*bodhisatta (Sanskrit: bodhisattva)*
>One who has a deep and spontaneous wish to become a
>Buddha for the benefit of all beings.

*brahmavihāra*
>The four "sublime states" or "divine abodes." They are *mettā*
>(friendliness, kindness, or goodwill), *karunā* (compassion),
>*muditā* (joy or appreciative joy), and *upekkhā* (equanimity).

Castaneda, Carlos*
>An anthropologist and author who wrote a series of books
>starting with *The Teachings of Don Juan* in 1968 about his
>training with a shaman in the Toltec lineage.

*cattāri ariya saccāni*
>The Four Noble Truths. These are the core of the Buddha's
>teaching. "Noble" refers not to the truths but to the mind that
>can perceive them correctly, so can also be translated as
>"ennobling." The Four Truths are *dukkha* (dissatisfaction or
>suffering), *tanhā* (tightness or craving), *nirodha* (cessation or the
>release of *tanhā*), and the Eightfold Path (*ariyo atthaṅgiko*
>*maggo*).

*Chachakka Sutta*
>One of the Buddha's talks (*Majjhima Nikāya* 148) that analyzes
>the six senses from six perspectives and shows how the self is
>"empty" and has no essence.

*chanda*
>Wholesome desire. Not all desires are all bad. Wanting to be
>more loving, compassionate, or generous are examples of
>wholesome desires. However, as the mind becomes more
>serene and receptive, all tightness that accompanies any kind
>of desire must be relaxed and released. Even wholesome
>desires can block the mind-heart's natural clarity from
>emerging.

clinging (see *upādāna*)

collectedness (see *samādhi*)

concentration
>Collectedness; calm abiding; stability of mind. The *Pāli* term
>*samādhi* is often translated as "concentration" because the

attention stays easily on an object. However, <u>samādhi</u> does not have the tension or strain that "concentration" may imply. It is collected and stable because there is little tension to pull it away. Forcing the mind to stay on one object creates tension, not <u>samādhi</u>.

contact (*see <u>phassa</u>*)

contemplate
> Observe. In English, the word "contemplate" often implies actively thinking about a topic. In the <u>suttas</u>, the <u>Pāli</u> word "contemplate" is usually a translation of a word like <u>sati,</u> which means merely to observe with an open awareness without cogitating upon it.

craving (see <u>taṇhā</u>)

dependent co-arising (see <u>paṭiccasamuppāda</u>)

dependent origination (see <u>paṭiccasamuppāda</u>)

*dhammā (Sanskrit: dharma)*
> The law, the way things are, the natural order. The term can also mean a phenomenon in and of itself, a mental quality, or a teaching. When capitalized, Dhamma refers to the teachings of the Buddha. To take refuge in the dhamma (lower case) means to take refuge in how things really are. To take refuge in the Dhamma (upper case) as a Buddhist monk does, is to rely on the Buddha's teachings.

*Dhammacakkappavattana Sutta*
> "The Discourse on Setting the Wheel of Dhamma in Motion," *Saṃyutta Nikāya* 56.11. In this text the Buddha gives his first successful teaching to his old meditation partners, the five ascetics. He explains the Middle Path and the Four Ennobling Truths.

*dharma*
> The Sanskrit spelling of <u>dhamma</u>.

*diṭṭhi (Sanskrit: dṛṣṭi)*
> View, perspective, or position. In Buddhism, a view or position is not a simple abstract proposition but a charged interpretation that can shape experience and thought. Right view or harmonious perspective (<u>sammā diṭṭhi</u>) is the first fold

or aspect of the Eightfold Path. It refers not so much to holding
a correct view as to having a way of seeing that is clear and
holds to no position. (See *ariyo aṭṭhaṅgiko maggo*.)

**Dōgen**
Dōgen Zenji was a thirteenth century monk, writer, poet, and
philosopher, and the founder of the Sōtō school of Zen
Buddhism in Japan.

*dosa*
Aversion; ill will; anger; hatred. *Dosa* is an urge to push
something away or to get away from something. It can be as
light as boredom or displeasure, or as strong as rage or disgust.

**downstream**
Following dependent origination (*paṭiccasamuppāda*) from
subtle to gross phenomena.

*dukkha*
Dissatisfaction, suffering, stress, discontent. *Dukkha* is the first
Ennobling Truth, which says that life has suffering. The
Buddha never said that life *is* suffering, only that nothing in the
relative world of constant change can be a reliable base for
constant happiness. A more colloquial translation of dukkha as
"bummer" conveys its wider range of meanings.

**eightfold path** (see *ariyo aṭṭhaṅgiko maggo*)

**emptiness**
No essence, soul, or core. Nothing (including the self) has an
essence that separates it from everything else. Emptiness
implies oneness because everything is connected with
everything else. (See *anattā*.)

**endear** (see *piyāsu*)

**ennobling** *(see cattāri ariya saccāni)*

**essence** *(see emptiness and anattā)*

**four noble (or ennobling) truths** (see *cattāri ariya saccāni*)

**four foundations** *(see Satipaṭṭhāna Sutta)*

Gautama
> The Buddha's family name or surname. By tradition, his first name was "Siddhārtha." However, this might have been a spiritual name given to him after his awakening.

Gendlin, Eugene*
> American author, philosopher, and psychotherapist best known for his book *Focusing,* which advocates for cultivating a direct "felt sense" of our experience unmediated by thought.

Gombrich, Richard*
> Indologist and scholar of Sanskrit, *Pāli*, and Buddhism who was a professor at the University of Oxford for 28 years and past president of the Pāli Text Society.

Hanson, Rick*
> Psychologist, writer, and student of Buddhism perhaps best known for his book *Buddha's Brain*.

*hetupaccayo*
> Causes and conditions. *Hetu* means a primary cause. *Paccayo* means a supporting condition that contributes to produce an effect. *Hetupaccayo* combines both meanings. Since there is no "and" in the word, it might be more precisely translated as "causeconditions."

hindrance *(see nīvarana)*

impersonal (see *anattā*)

imponderables *(see acinteyya)*

*jarāmarana*
> The final "downstream" event in the flow of dependent origination *(paticcasamuppāda). Jarā* literally means "old age." *Marana* literally means "death." *Jarāmarana* refers to the "whole mass of suffering": sorrow, lamentation, pain, grief, and despair.

*jāti*
> Birth, or birth of action. The term traditionally refers to the arising of a new entity. In dependent origination *(paticcasamuppāda)*, it can also refer to the beginning of a mental, verbal, or physical action.

*jhāna*
> A stage of meditative knowledge gained through direct experience. The nature of the jhānas and how to work with them is discussed in detail in *Buddha's Map*[41] and elsewhere.

Kabir*
> A fifteenth-century Indian mystic poet whose writings were mostly concerned with devotion, mysticism, and discipline.

*kalahā*
> Quarrels.

*kāya*
> Body. *Kāya* refers to the material body alone — what is present in a corpse. *Rūpa* refers to a living body.

*khandha* (Sanskrit: skandha)
> Aggregate; heap; cluster. The five khandha (body, feeling tone, perception, concepts and storylines, and consciousness or awareness) refer to the various phenomena people often identify as "self." In this context they are often called "aggregates affected by clinging." All five khandha together include everything we can experience.

Kosambi
> A great city in the time of the Buddha. Several Buddhist monasteries were in the vicinity of Kosambi. A great schism among the monks of Kosambi is described in the early texts.

*kuti*
> A small hut used for meditation.

Lao Tzu*
> An ancient Chinese philosopher and writer and the reputed author of the *Tao Te Ching* and founder of Taoism. He may have been a contemporary of the Buddha, but there is no direct evidence that the two knew each other.

link (see *nidāna*)

---

[41] Doug Kraft, "Six Rs: The Real Practice," *Buddha's Map*.

*lobha*
> Sensory or sensual desire. It can be as light as quiet yearning or as strong as greed or craving. It is an urge to have something or to move toward something.

*Maggasamyutta*
> *Samyutta Nikāya* 41.2(2), in which the Buddha declares the value of good friends and companions on the spiritual journey.

*Mahātaṇhāsankhaya Sutta*
> The "Discourse on the Destruction of Craving" (*Majjhima Nikāya* 38.14) in which the fisherman, Sati, promotes the view that the same soul migrates from one life time to another and the Buddha chastises him through a lengthy description of dependent origination (*paticcasamuppāda*).

*Majjhima Nikāya*
> The Middle Length Discourses of the Buddha. The *Pāli Canon* is a collection of over 10,000 *suttas* or discourses attributed to the Buddha or his chief disciples. It is divided into three *pitakas* ("baskets"). The second basket, the *Sutta Pitaka*, is divided into five *nikāyas* (collections). The *Majjhima Nikāya* is the second of the five. It contains 152 suttas. They provide a comprehensive body of teaching concerning all aspects of the Buddha's teachings.

Mara
> Mara is depicted as a demon who tried to seduce the Buddha in various ways, always failing. Mara is described as "the personification of forces antagonistic to awakening."

*maîtrī (see metta)*

*maraṇa (see jarāmaraṇa)*

Meister Eckhart*
> German theologian, philosopher, and mystic (c. 1260–1328).

*mettā (Sanskrit: maîtrī)*
> Loving kindness, goodwill, and gentle friendship. *Mettā* is the first of the four sublime states (*brahmavihāras*) the Buddha recommended be cultivated. These can be very effective objects of meditation. Mettā is usually translated as "loving kindness," but a more accurate rendering is "friendliness."

*mindfulness (see <u>sati</u>)*

mind-heart
> Buddhism does not make the distinction between mind and
> heart often made in the West. I use the term mind-heart to refer
> to all those qualities together.

mindstream
> That which may pass from one body to the next. Various
> religious traditions use the term in different ways. Some say
> the mindstream carries memories and impressions from one
> lifetime to the next. It should not be confused with soul or self,
> because our sense of self is made up of many transient
> phenomena.

*moha*
> Confusion, lack of clarity, delusion. This might be caused by
> anything from bad information to a deranged mind.

*muditā*
> Joy, especially but not exclusively the joy that arises from
> seeing someone's good fortune. Muditā is the third of the four
> sublime states (<u>*brahmavihāras*</u>) and can be a very effective
> meditation object.

*nāmarūpa*
> Mind-body. As a phase of <u>dependent origination</u>
> (<u>*paṭiccasamuppāda*</u>), it refers to a condition before mind and
> body has arisen as separate phenomena. Mind (*nāma*) and
> body (<u>*rūpa*</u>) are said to co-arise.

*nibbāna (Sanskrit: nirvāṇa)*
> Extinguished. The word literally means "blown out" as in a
> candle that is extinguished. In the scientific thinking of the
> Buddha's time, when a fire goes out, the heat element in the
> flame does not go away. It simply ceases to cling to the burning
> object: it disperses. To those who heard the Buddha use the
> term, it meant the complete cessation of craving and clinging.
> Through meditation training, we can relax so deeply that all
> perception and consciousness cease for a period of time.
> Coming out of this state, we can see <u>dependent origination</u>
> (<u>*paṭiccasamuppāda*</u>) so clearly that we no longer identify with

psychophysical processes. When this is deep and full enough, we wake up.

*nibbidā*
Disenchantment. When we see the truth of how the things actually operate, the enchantment or attachment to the world fades. At first this can be quite disturbing. But as the experience deepens, it moves toward dispassion.

*nidāna*
Link. A *Pāli* term that is a synonym for *hetupaccayo* (causes and conditions). However, it is usually translated as "link" when referring to <u>dependent origination</u> (*paticcasamuppāda*) because it links adjacent factors. It is also sometimes translated as "cause" or "condition."

*nikāya*
Volume; collection; assemblage; class. *Nikāya* most commonly refers to one of the five collections of the *suttas* that make up the *Pāli Canon*. The five are the <u>*Dīgha Nikāya*</u> (long discourses), the <u>*Majjhima Nikāya*</u> (middle-length discourses), the *Saṃyutta Nikāya* (thematically linked discourses), *Aṅguttara Nikāya* (the discourses grouped by content enumeration), and the *Khuddaka Nikāya* (minor or shorter discourses).

*nirodha*
Cessation, absence, or extinction. Nirodha is the third of the Four Noble Truths, which points to the cessation of perception, feeling, and consciousness. With this is the cessation of suffering.

*nirvāṇa* (see *nibbāna*)

*nīvaraṇa*
Hindrance; veil; something that gets in the way of meditation progress. The term literally means a covering – it covers something valuable. So the problem is not what we perceive but how we relate to it. If we are skillful, we can use *nīvaraṇa* to point out something that needs wise attention. The <u>Six Rs</u> are the best way to work with hindrances and turn them to our advantage.

nondual
"Not two;" oneness. A mature state of consciousness in which the dichotomy of self and other fades: there is no distinction between what is known and the knower.

non-self *(see anattā)*

nothingness
The seventh jhāna where external references fade into the background and all that's left are subjective experiences. It might be better translated as "no thingness" since there are no external things.

Nye, Naomi Shihab*
A poet, songwriter, and novelist, born to a Palestinian father and an American mother, who grew up in St. Louis, Jerusalem, and San Antonio, Texas.

Pāli
The language used in recording the *suttas* and many early texts. It was close to the language the Buddha spoke (*Prakrit*), but not actually the same.

*Pāli Canon (see Sutta Pitaka)*
A collection of over 10,000 suttas or discourses attributed to the Buddha or his chief disciples. It is divided into three pitakas ("baskets")

*pamāda*
Heedlessness; carelessness; negligence that leads to moral lapse.

*paññā*
Wisdom; insight; seeing into the true nature or reality. In Buddhism it has the more specific meaning of understanding dependent origination (see *paticcasamuppāda*).

*papañca*
Wandering thoughts; discursive mind.

*passaddhi*
Calmness, tranquility, serenity. It is the seventh awakening factor and is part of the so-called "higher path" of dependent origination (*paticcasamuppāda*) that describes the process of awakening.

*paṭiccasamuppāda (Sanskrit: pratītyasamutpāda)*
> Dependent co-arising or dependent origination. This is the central teaching of the Buddha about how everything arises because of causes and conditions. Seeing this clearly is central to his path of awakening. "Dependent origination" is the more literal translation and implies that causes are connected to effects as much as effects to causes.

*phassa*
> Raw uninterpreted sensation. It's often called "contact," meaning contact between a sensation (e.g., light), a sensory organ (e.g., an eye), and sensory awareness (e.g., seeing).

*pitaka*
> Literally "basket." The Buddha's discourses were originally recorded on leaves and collected into three pitaka or baskets know as Vinaya, Sutta, and Abhidamma.

*piya*
> Dear; amiable, beloved.

Prakrit
> An ancient Indian language that has many dialects. *Prakrit* means "natural," "normal," "artless," or "vernacular" as contrasted to the more literary and religious orthodoxy of Sanskrit. The Buddha probably spoke a dialect of *Prakrit* called *Ardhamāgadhi* ("half-Magadhi." Magadhi was a major city in the Buddha's time).

pure awareness
> Awareness without an agenda or tension; awareness of awareness itself.

*rūpa*
> Body, physical phenomenon, sense information. It has different meanings in different contexts. For example, as a sensory object, *rūpa* is the object of the sense of sight. As the first khandha, it is physical phenomena or sensations picked by sensory organs. In "nāmarūpa," it means physical as opposed to mental phenomena (*nāma*).

*saddhā (Sanskrit: śraddhā)*
  Confidence, faith. In some contexts, it means faith in the Buddha's path. It is part of the so-called "higher path" of dependent origination (*paticcasamuppāda*) that describes the process of awakening. With stream entry (the beginning of awakening), it becomes unshakable.

*samādhi*
  Collectedness, calm abiding. Often it is translated as concentration or one-pointedness. But it has neither the strain implied by "concentration" nor the blocking out of other phenomena as implied by "one-pointedness." It is a unified and quiet quality of consciousness. *Samādhi* is one of the awakening factors as well as part of the eightfold path (*ariyo atthangiko maggo*).

*sammā*
  Harmonious, skillful, wise. In the context of the eightfold path (*ariyo atthangiko maggo*), it is often translated as "right." But the *Pāli* term does not carry the sense of right and wrong or good and bad implied in English. The name of each aspect of the eightfold path starts with "sammā."

*sammā ditthi*
  Wise view. The first fold of eightfold path (*ariyo atthangiko maggo*).

*sampajañña*
  Commonly translated as "clear comprehension" or "clear knowing," *sampajañña* means knowing what's going on in the moment and knowing the larger context at the same time. It's like a wide-angle lens that sees both depth and breadth.

*samsāra*
  The world and the suffering found in it. The word literally means "continuous flow" and refers to the continuous flow from birth to life to death to rebirth.

*samudaya*
  Origin, source. It is the second Noble Truth, which refers to the origin of dissatisfaction (*dukkha*).

*Saṃyutta Nikāya*
> The Connected Discourses. This <u>nikāya</u> is part of the <u>Pāli</u> Cannon. This collection of over 10,000 <u>suttas</u> (discourses) is attributed to the Buddha or his chief disciples. It is divided into three <u>pitakas</u> ("baskets"). The second basket, the <u>Sutta Pitaka</u>, is divided into five <u>nikāyas</u> (collections). The *Saṃyutta Nikāya* is the third of the five. The suttas are grouped into five avgas (sections), each of which is further divided into *saṃyuttas* (chapters) on related topics.

*saṅgha*
> Originally it referred to the community of Buddhist monks and nuns. Today it is often used to refer to any community of people dedicated to the Buddha's teachings.

*Sanskrit*
> A primary language of Hinduism, Sikhism, Jainism, and Buddhism. It is a scholarly language used in liturgy and scholarship. The relationship between Sanskrit and <u>Pāli</u> is similar to the relationship between Latin and Italian.

*saṅkhāra*
> Thoughts, concepts, storylines, or anything else that has been mentally formed or put together. Saṅkhāra is a complex term that is used in lots of different ways. *Khāra* means "action." *Saṅ-* puts added emphasis on it. So the word is often translated as "volitional formations." But this can be confusing in English. "Volitional" in English implies conscious intention or even willpower. But the <u>Pāli</u> term can imply unconscious inclinations and tendencies. And "formation" in English implies something solid and lasting. But in Buddhism the sense is fragility — anything that has been put together or formed falls apart. (See <u>volition</u>.)

*saññā (Sanskrit: saṃjñā)*
> Perception, label. It is seen as a subtle but active process whereby we compare an experience to our past experiences and figure out what it is (i.e., what to label it).

Sarnath
A small town not far from Varanasi. It was here in the Deer
Park that the Buddha first taught the <u>*Dhamma*</u> to five ascetics
who had been companions of his before his enlightenment.

*sātam asātanti* (or *sāta/asātanti*)
The bare feeling tone of pleasing (*sātam*) and unpleasing
(*asātanti*). These two terms are used in the earliest Buddhist
text. The later text uses one word, <u>*vedanā*,</u> instead.

*sati (Sanskrit: smṛti)*
<u>Mindfulness,</u> heartfulness, the state of being fully present
without habitual reactions. It is a very important quality in
Buddhist practice. The <u>*Pāli*</u> language does not make a
distinction between mind and heart, so sati includes both these
qualities. It is the balancing factor of the seven <u>awakening
factors</u>. It is also the seventh aspect of the Eightfold Path. (See
<u>*ariyo aṭṭhaṅgiko maggo*,</u> the Noble Eightfold Path.)

*Satipaṭṭhāna Sutta*
The "Discourse on the Foundation of Mindfulness," *Majjhima
Nikāya* 10. The four foundations are mindfulness of four
domains: physical sensation, feeling tone (<u>*vedanā*</u>), mind or
consciousness (*citta*), and mind-objects (*dhammās*). This <u>*sutta*</u> is
considered by many <u>*Theravada*</u> Buddhists to be the core of the
Buddha's teachings.

*Sayadaw*
A Burmese Buddhist title for a senior monk or abbot of a
monastery, or for a highly respected teacher.

Sayadaw U Tejaniya*
A <u>Theravadin</u> Buddhist monk of Burmese-Chinese lineage
whose teachings have attracted a global audience for his clarity
and sense of humor.

selfing
The mental process of creating or strengthening the sense of
having a self or self-essence that sets one fundamentally apart
from the web of life. The Buddha said this is a persistent
delusion.

Shantideva*

An eight-century Buddhist monk who trained at the Buddhist university at Nalanda, India. He is renowned for writing *The Way of the Bodhisattva,* a long poem that describes the process of enlightenment from first thought to full Buddhahood.

Siddhārtha

*Siddha* means "accomplished" and *artha* means "goal." *Siddhārtha* means "one who accomplished his goal." By tradition, this was the Buddha's first name. However, it is more likely that it was a spiritual name by which he was referred to after his awakening.

*Six Rs*

A six-phase technique used in meditation and all of life to deal wisely with distractions and disturbances in the <u>mind-heart</u>. Its effectiveness comes from its simplicity and its foundation in what the Buddha called Wise Effort, or <u>*sammā*</u> <u>*vāyāma*</u> (see pp. 17-19).

sloth

Loss of motivation. Sloth and <u>torpor</u> together are one of the five main hindrances.

*sutta (Sanskrit: sūtra)*

A talk given by the Buddha. The *suttas* are part of the canonical text. The term literally means "thread." The implication is that to understand the "whole cloth" of the <u>*Dhamma*</u>, it's important to know how the suttas are woven together.

*Sutta Nipata*

A collection of <u>*suttas*</u> that is part of the *Khuddaka Nikāya* (collection of shorter suttas). Many scholars believe these may be some of the earliest suttas.

*Sutta Pitaka (Sanskrit: Sūtra Pitaka)*

Literally it means "basket of discourses." It is the second of three division of the *Tripitaka* or *Pāli Canon* and contains about 10,000 <u>*suttas*</u>.

*taṇhā (Sanskrit: tṛṣṇā)*

Craving, tightness, holding. Though *taṇhā* is most often translated as "craving," it can be very subtle. It is a preverbal tightening as we try to avoid something uncomfortable, hang on to something pleasurable, or space out with something neutral. The Buddha identified it as the "weak link" in dependent origination (*paticcasamuppāda*) — the easiest place to stop the "downstream" of events by relaxing the tightness. Besides being the eighth phase of dependent origination, it is subtly present in all phases as well as being the second of the *cattāri ariya saccāni* (Four Ennobling Truths).

Tejaniya*
See Sayadaw U Tejaniya.

*Theravada*
*Theravada* literally means "school of the elder monks." It uses the Buddha's Teachings in the *Pāli* Canon as its primary source. It is probably best known for insight meditation (*vipassanā).*

torpor
Dull or sleepy awareness. Sloth and torpor together are one of the five main hindrances.

*Udāna*
A collection of 80 Buddhist suttas that is part of the *Pāli Canon*. The word *udāna* means "inspired utterance." Each *sutta* has an utterance preceded by a narrative to give it context. Scholars believe the utterances may actually go back to the Buddha.

*upādāna*
Clinging; the way the mind shrink-wraps around a thought or perception. It is always experienced as thinking or the beginning of thinking. It is the seventh phase of dependent origination (*paticcasamuppāda*). It arises when *tanhā* is not relaxed and released.

*veda*
Veda literally means "knowledge." The Vedas are a large body of texts originating in ancient India.

*vedanā*
Feeling tone. *Vedanā* can be pleasant, painful, or neither. It arises out of raw perception.

Venerable
A title or word used to refer to an ordained Buddhist monk.

*via negativa*
> A way of describing something by saying what it is not. It is associated with mysticism and non-ordinary perception.

*vicāra*
> The kind of thinking that wisely discerns. For example, in meditation if a small distraction arises, you may decide whether it is minor enough to ignore or if you should Six-R it. *Vicāra* is the type of thinking that skillfully decides what to do. It is not the wondering or free associational kind of thinking. (Compare to *papañca*.)

Vimalaraṁsi
> See Bhante Vimalaraṁsi

*viññāṇa*
> Consciousness; awareness; bare cognition. Consciousness is in flux and does not constitute an abiding mind-substance, soul, or transmigrating entity. It arises when the conditions are right. It can be one of six kinds according to the sense it is associated with.

*vivādā*
> Disputes.

wholesome / unwholesome
> Wholesome qualities are ones that are beneficial. They have little tension in them or tend to reduce tension. Unwholesome qualities are not beneficial. They have tension or increase tension.

wisdom
> Seeing the causal relationships in dependent origination (*paticcasamuppāda*). In English, the word "wisdom" has a broad meaning. When the Buddha used the word, he was always referring to seeing the causal relationships. Seeing them is the core of the *Dhamma*. (See *paññā*.)

yogi
> A person who sincerely follows a spiritual path that includes a discipline like meditation. Narrowly, the term refers to someone proficient in yoga. However the term more broadly includes any sincere meditator.

# Index

Note: **bold page numbers indicate primary entries**, *italic numbers indicate quotations*, underlined entries have glossary definitions.

Printed in Great Britain
by Amazon